AF225762

Spirituality for the Solitary

Spirituality for the Solitary

A Handbook for Those Who Live Alone

Mark G. Boyer

WIPF & STOCK · Eugene, Oregon

Dedicated to
Marcia Jones,
a friend and a spiritual solitary.

"... [T]he world as we know it is our interpretation
of observable facts in the light of theories of our own
invention. . . . [W]e invent our world even while we
think we are just observing it and reporting on it."

—ROBERT F. TAFT, "BETWEEN"

"I am struck by the *new in the old*. . . . I now realize and
appreciate the difficulty and commitment it takes to preserve a
history. . . . [T]he way of preservation comes not by maintaining a
hands-off approach; instead, it is a creative and active process."

—JEFFREY ROBBINS, "DISPATCHES"

Contents

Abbreviations | ix

Introduction | xi

1   Prayer | 1

2   Celebrations that Enhance Spirituality | 38
   Water, Food and Drink, Oil, Hands, Incense, Soil (Dirt),
   Oak Tree, Dog, Lamp (Light), Clothing, Ring, Fire, Wind,
   Music, House, Generic Celebration | 99

3   Conclusion | 104

Bibliography | 109

Recent Books by Mark G. Boyer published by Wipf & Stock | 115

Abbreviations

BCE = Before the Common Era (same as BC = Before Christ)

CB (NT) = Christian Bible (New Testament)

    Acts = Acts of the Apostles
    John = John's Gospel
    Luke = Luke's Gospel
    Mark = Mark's Gospel
    Matt = Matthew's Gospel
    Rev = Revelation
    1 Thess = First Letter of Paul to the Thessalonians

CE = Common Era (same as AD = *Anno Domini*, in the year of
    the Lord)

HB (OT) = Hebrew Bible (Old Testament)

    Amos = Amos
    1 Chr = First Book of Chronicles
    2 Chr = Second Book of Chronicles
    Dan = Daniel
    Exod = Exodus
    Ezek = Ezekiel
    Gen = Genesis
    Isa = Isaiah
    Josh = Joshua

Judg = Judges
1 Kgs = First Book of Kings
2 Kgs = Second Book of Kings
Lam = Lamentations
Lev = Leviticus
Num = Numbers
Prov = Proverbs
Ps(s) = Psalm(s)
1 Sam = First Book of Samuel
2 Sam = Second Book of Samuel

OT (A) = Old Testament (Apocrypha)

Sg Three = Prayer of Azariah (Song of Three Jews)
Sir = Sirach (Ecclesiasticus)
Tob = Tobit

par(s) = paragraph(s)

Introduction

Title: *Spirituality for the Solitary*

Solitary

T HIS IS A BOOK about spirituality, more specifically, spirituality for the solitary. The solitaries are those who live alone. In history they are known as hermits, eremites, anchorites, and solitaries. Today, they are known as pioneers, mountain men and women, widows, widowers, and people who choose to live alone in the country or in the city. The pandemic of 2019 to 2022 made solitaries out of anyone who stayed home alone to avoid COVID, flu, a cold, and other viruses. The image associated with historical hermits, eremites, and anchorites is spending all day in prayer in a cabin in the woods, mountains, or deserts. However, today such a solitary spends most of the day doing chores, like cooking, cleaning, walking and feeding the dog, cutting wood for fire, going to work, etc. Some times of the day—especially morning and evening—may be spent in prayer and meditation.

The solitary life continues to be lived and illustrated on the History Channel's *Mountain Men* series. The solitary life is still alive and well across the United States, especially in Alaska. Sam Keith made Richard Proenneke's move to the forty-ninth state's wilderness, cabin building, and daily life famous in his book *One Man's Wilderness*, which became Bob Swerer's documentary *Alone in the Wilderness* and *Alone in the Wilderness: Part II* about Proenneke's thirty-year adventure as a solitary. John Krakauer's *Into the Wild* demonstrates the desire of Christopher McCandless to live a solitary, self-sustaining life in the Alaskan wilderness without the necessary survival skills that results in tragedy. Sean Penn turned Krakauer's book into a screenplay and directed the film by the same name. In the mid-1960s, Vardis Fisher popularized the solitary life in his novel *Mountain Man*. In the early 1970s Robert Redford, directed by Sydney Pollack, further popularized the solitary life in *Jeremiah Johnson*, the film version of Fisher's book.

Personally, I met Bill Rambo, a solitary living in a shack in the Little Dominquez River canyon in Colorado. He raised goats for milk and meat, and he made two trips a year to the closest town to buy beans and rice, to vote, and to go to the local library to get free books. He lived alone for thirty years cultivating fruit trees, cutting fire wood, repairing his home, and keeping up with the world beyond the canyon through his computer, whose batteries he recharged using a gasoline electric generator.

People like Rambo choose to live alone for all kinds of reasons. Most spirituality is geared to community, but solitaries do not want or need others to enhance their spirituality. They are not community-minded, nor group oriented, nor anti-social; they are independent, except for the dog or cat who may live with them.

The solitary prays; it is prayer and not worship, which implies praying with others. There is no congregation, church building, minister, etc. The solitary's place of prayer is his or her place of living. Thus, prayer and living and all that is associated with both are intertwined. In community, according to Joyce Zimmerman, "Worship . . . leads to a kind of spirituality, a certain way of living."[1] Where there is no community worship, however, there can be spirituality for the solitary. Donald Braxton writes, "The concept of

---

1. Zimmerman, *Worship*, 126.

spirituality has become a concept without a home in the modern world."[2] While Braxton writes, ". . . [T]he rug has been pulled from underneath the traditional functions of religion and the case for religion has been weakened in all societies where science is pursued with any rigor,"[3] because religion is founded on membership, laws of belonging, attendance, commandments, tradition, unchangeableness, the solitary, who by definition is not interested in all of that, needs non-traditional spirituality. Furthermore, many forms of religion focus on sin, on how bad people are—"Jesus died for my sins"—whereas positive solitary spirituality is focused on how good people are—"Jesus showed me how to be whole, wholly (holy) human."

Kevin Anderson points out that the *Dhammapada,* the collected sayings of the Buddha, begins: "We are what we think. All that we are arises with our thoughts. With our thoughts we make the world."[4] Anderson explains: ". . . [H]abitual thoughts create our habitual emotions, which in turn create our habitual behaviors. . . . [H]ow hard it is for most people to find new, healthier thoughts that lead them to more solid ground."[5]

Kristie Klussman refers to this as not having a sense of purpose. According to her, people fall into one of three categories: "the disengaged, the dreamers, and the dabblers."[6] She explains: "The disengaged are not passionate about anything beyond themselves and their own enjoyment and give no signs that they are interested in finding a purposeful pursuit. The dreamers have ideas about how they might find a life of meaning, but they have [not] developed any practical, realistic plan to make those ideas a reality. The dabblers are engaged in activities that might be purposeful, but they jump from thing to thing without sustained commitment— an essential aspect of finding purpose."[7]

2. Braxton, "Religion," 4.

3. Braxton, "Religion," 4.

4. Anderson, "Thistle," 19.

5. Anderson, "Thistle," 19.

6. Klussman, "What's," 38.

7. Klussman, "What's," 38.

The spiritual solitary demonstrates his or her sense of purpose through self-preservation. That is why the practice of solitary spirituality appears in Buddhism, Jainism, Hinduism, Sufism, and Taoism along with Judaism and Christianity. The solitary seeks solitude for meditation, contemplative prayer, self-awareness, and personal development. A part of the spiritual solitary's lifestyle may include a simplified diet and manual labor as a means of support or sustaining the self. Today, we find solitaries in man caves and she sheds. Some may own a lake house, a mountain house, or a country house. Some may rent an apartment. Those are the modern places solitaries inhabit.

In Judaism, the best examples of biblical solitaries are the eighth-century BCE prophets Elijah and Elisha, whose stories are imbedded in the Frist and Second Book of Kings in the Bible. As I explained in *From Contemplation to Action,* "They appear in activity when they are needed, and they disappear into solitude and silence when they are not."[8] Another biblical solitary is John the Baptist. According to Mark's Gospel, he "appeared in the wild, preaching a baptism of life-change" (Mark 1:4). Using Mark's Gospel as one of his sources, the author of Matthew's Gospel states that John the Baptist "was preaching in the desert country of Judea" (Matt 3:1). And the author of Luke's Gospel, also using Mark's Gospel as one of his sources, writes John the Baptist "was out in the desert," where he "received a message from God" and was "preaching a baptism of life-change" (Luke 3:2–3). The preaching about life change to others came through the life change John the Baptist discovered living a solitary life in the desert.

In the late fifth and early sixth Century CE, Benedict of Nursia lived alone in a cave above a lake for three years. Later, he wrote a rule (guide) for solitary monks forming a community. In chapter 1 of his *Rule,* Benedict lists hermits among the four kinds of monks existing at his time. He states: ". . . [T]he anchorites or hermits: those who, no longer in the first fervor of their reformation, but after long probation in a monastery, having learned by the help of many brethren . . ., go out well armed from the ranks of the

8. Boyer, *From Contemplation,* xxiii.

community to the solitary combat of the desert. They are able now, with no help save from God, to fight single-handed against the vices of the flesh and their own evil thoughts."[9] The word *monk* and its derivative words—*monastery, monastic, monasticism*—come into English through the Greek word *monazein*, which means "to live alone." The prefix *mono*, which appears in many English words, means *one, single, alone.* Thus, by the late fifth and early sixth centuries CE, there were monks living in monasteries with a rule under the leadership of an abbot, and there were solitaries, who lived alone after being formed in a monastery. There were some solitaries who lived alone without having first been formed in a monastery; Benedict does not have anything good to say about them! Benedict did not invent monasticism; he gave it some order. Those called hermits, from the Greek word *eremites*, meaning *of the desert*, were solitaries who lived in caves, cells, or hermitages in the desert or in forests. Such a forest hermit was St. Meinrad, who lived at the time of Charlemagne (747–814 CE). His hermitage was a hut in a mountain forest where he lived for twenty-six years and where he was killed by robbers. His pet ravens followed the thieves and alerted authorities, who arrested them for their crimes. Bruno of Cologne (1030–1101 CE) preferred the solitary life; he founded the Carthusian Order, who like the Camaldolese—another religious order—arrange their monasteries as clusters of hermitages in which monks live most of their days and lives in solitary prayer and work. A famous woman anchoress—from the Greek *anakhorein*, meaning *to withdraw*—was Julian of Norwich (1343–1416 CE), who lived in a cell (sealed room) attached to St. Julian Church for most of her adult life. These are but a few of the many men and women of the past who lived a spiritually solitary life. In modern times, there are many men and women of all religions and those not practicing any religion living alone and seeking deeper spirituality. They no longer go to a desert or forest and build a hermitage or live in a cave, and they certainly no longer get themselves sealed in a room attached to a church! They

9. Benedict, *St. Benedict's Rule*, 6.

live in houses and apartments; they do not make vows, but live an eremitic lifestyle as monks, hermits, anchorites, and solitaries.

Christine Paintner references John Cassian (360–435 CE), a monk, when writing about spiritual journey. According to Painter, Cassian presents three renunciations which apply to solitary spirituality. The first renunciation "is our former way of life . . . . The second is the inner practice of asceticism and letting go of our mindless thoughts. The third renunciation is to let go of our image of God and to recognize that any image or pronouncement we can ever make about God is much too small to contain the divine."[10]

Renouncing the former way of life means leaving family and home and moving to a house or apartment. For most people this occurs after high school or college. There is a desire within the solitary to live alone, to have no housemates. Alone, a person in the beginning most likely lives with only the bare essentials in austerity; in order to have what is needed to stay alive, he or she may practice a mild form of self-denial. This ascetic way of life is not filled with distractions. Thus, thoughts are not mindless; they are focused and required for survival. A solitary who thinks about the divine may begin to recognize that whatever can be said about God is always inadequate. It is impossible to capture God in words. Sometimes saying nothing is saying all! Just beginning to live alone in a house or apartment begins to transform one's life. Richard Rohr calls this a crossover moment, "after which a person will never be the same again. Somewhere, somehow the challenge comes that sets us on a different path: the path of purpose, the path of integrity, the path of transcendence that lifts us—heart, mind, and soul—above the pitiable level of the comfortable and the mundane."[11] As we settle into our new ordered life, a new feeling of life-is-good envelopes us. It is OK to be who we have become because of our solitude. We may have a greater knowledge of our identity; we may feel more secure as we continue to live our new solitary lives.

Whether or not we realize it, from a spiritual perspective, we can attribute the transformation to God, the divine presence. We

10. Paintner, *Soul*, 114.

11. Rohr, "Politics."

may not have considered our living alone to have anything to do with the divine or the spiritual, but just because we did not recognize God's presence doesn't mean that the divine was not there! Because we exist in the very One—no matter what name we give— all is done in the divine presence. There is no need to identify ourselves as a hermit, eremitic, or anchorite, as is often done by overtly religious people! It makes no difference if we awaken to the divine presence in whom we live and move and have our being. Transformation occurs because we cooperate with God, whether we are aware of it or not. In spiritual solitariness, God transforms us.

In "The Gospel of Thomas," an apocryphal sayings gospel dated between 60 and 250 CE, Jesus says: "Blessed are the solitary . . . , for you will find the kingdom. For you are from it, and you will return there again" (49). Later, he adds, "Many are standing at the door, but only the solitary will enter the bridal chamber" (75).[12]

STOP/MEDITATE/JOURNAL: Throughout this book, sections of Stop/Meditate/Journal are presented to help the solitary apply the material just read to his or her spirituality. It is important to stop consuming the text. Meditate or reflect on the questions that follow, and record your reflections, thoughts, and prayers in a journal in order to trace your growth in solitary spirituality.

1. What image of God do you need to release?

2. What way of your previous life do you need to release?

3. What activities do you need to release to have time for meditation, contemplation, and prayer?

12. "Gospel of Thomas," 58, 63.

Spirituality

This book presents *spirituality* for the solitary. As an adjective, the word, *spiritual*, basically, refers to aspects of one's spirit. I prefer the word *spirit* over *soul* because spirit is more biblical—("God formed Man out of dirt from the ground and blew into his nostrils the breath of life," Gen 2:7)—while soul is more philosophical, specifically Socratic, Platonic, and Aristotelian. Throughout this book you will encounter the word *soul*, as it appears in quotations; I urge you to substitute the word *spirit*. Michael Hanson narrates an Israelite belief in this regard: ". . . [W]hen a child is born, the child's first breath takes in the breath that the Creator has just breathed out. When the person dies and breathes his or her last breath out, the Creator breathes it in and eternal life begins."[13] In both Hebrew and Greek, the word for breath and spirit is the same word: *ruah, pneuma*. Stefanos Alexopoulos and Maxwell E. Johnson remind us that the Holy Spirit "is everywhere [and] fills all places, and no place contains him."[14] Spirituality is the practice of awareness that each person's spirit is connected to Spirit.

The noun *spirituality,* refers to the quality or condition of being spiritual, that is, being in touch with or aware of one's spirit connected to Spirit and nurturing it. Rami Shapiro begins with an understanding that all is in God. Known as panentheism, Shapiro teaches that we already exist in the divine. Everything and everyone are in God. "Everything is an expression of a dynamic process called by many names—God, Mother, Brahman, Allah, YHH, Tao, Kali, etc.," writes Shapiro.[15] "We live and move in him," states the author of the Acts of the Apostles; we "can't get away from him!" (Acts 17:28). The same author explained through Jesus in Luke's Gospel that Moses "at the burning bush, saying, 'God: God of Abraham, God of Isaac, God of Jacob!' God isn't the God of dead men, but of the living. To him all are alive" (Luke 20:37–38).[16]

13. Hansen, *First*, 231.

14. Alexopoulos and Johnson, *Introduction*, 96.

15. Shapiro, "Roadside Assistance," *Spirituality and Health* 25:1 (2022) 9.

16. The author of Luke's Gospel got this account from his Markan Gospel source. The Markan Jesus states, "How God at the bush said to Moses, 'I

By the time of Moses, Abraham, Isaac, and Jacob had been dead for a long time. What the Lukan Jesus explains is that people do not go out of existence with death, because they are alive in God throughout life, and they stay alive in God even in death. Whatever and whomever exist cannot exist outside the divine nor go out of existence. God is pure existence (being); all is spirit. All people, animals, trees, etc.—even those extinct—are alive in God. Thus, Shapiro writes, "Spirituality isn't fixed but fluid, not a final 'aha' but a recurring 'wow.'"[17] Gerhard Lohfink explains, "God is ungraspable and far beyond all our ideas and windy words."[18] "God (with a capital 'G') is the infinite Aliveness," states Shapiro, "manifesting all reality. You don't worship God; you awaken in, with, and as God."[19] Gregory Boyle comes to the same conclusion, writing, ". . . [T]he Lord comes to us disguised as ourselves" as we "learn to pay better attention."[20] Alexander Turpin reminds us, ". . . [W]e can access the unlimited God anywhere, anytime."[21] Shapiro continues: "Knowing this . . . reveals the sacredness of all life and the preconsciousness of each life. Knowing this . . . leads to living the Golden Rule and to loving neighbor and stranger as a part of your Self (Lev 19:18, 34). Knowing this . . . leads you beyond tribalism and religious competition. Knowing this . . . doesn't erase the value of religion, but it does provide a means for evaluating religion. Any religion that reveals this . . . is of value. Any religion that doesn't, isn't."[22] Today, many people think religion is broken; it is controlled by leadership that has stripped it of its spirituality and replaced it

---

am—not *was*—the God of Abraham, the God of Isaac, and the God of Jacob? The living God is God of the living, not the dead" (Mark 12:26–27). The author of Matthew's Gospel also uses Mark's Gospel as his source for the same account. Matthew records Jesus saying: "The grammar is clear: God says, 'I am—not *was*—the God of Abraham, the God of Isaac, the God of Jacob.' The living God defines himself not as the God of dead men, but of the living" (Matt 22:32).

17. Shapiro, "Roadside Assistance: Holy Land," 47.

18. Lohfink, *Between*, 123.

19. Shapiro, "Roadside Assistance," *Spirituality and Health* 25:6 (2022) 8.

20. Boyle, *Tattoos*, 60.

21. Turpin, "Of Pandemics," 335.

22. Shapiro, "Roadside Assistance," *Spirituality and Health* 25:1 (2022) 9.

with membership, laws of belonging, and commandments. Furthermore, the use of electronic media of all kinds by churches have catered to the person at home and contributed to the creation of solitaries; if one can watch spirituality-lacking religious services on TV, why attend them with others? The flexibility religion needs to nourish spirituality is gone; the process of spirituality has ceased. "The concept of spirituality has become a concept without a home in the modern world," states Donald Braxton.[23] People wanting spirituality get only more religion, and so they leave the churches that should be supplying spirituality. Because human beings are naturally—in terms of being in God, the source of spirit and Spirit—spiritual, nature, as we will see below, becomes "a true exemplification and instantiation of grace."[24] But many churches seem to have forgotten that point.

Thus, Shapiro writes that spirituality is "the art of exploring [our] nature. . . . [I]t is a direct apprehension of reality outside of words and scripture; a direct pointing to reality and seeing into one's true nature."[25] Lohfink seems to agree, writing, "In reality the human being is an utterly insignificant speck of dust in a cold and empty universe, but the 'supernaturally inclined' refuse to accept that."[26] Shapiro adds, "The closer you get to death the clearer your understanding of life becomes."[27] The big picture presents divine life everywhere. Becoming aware of it is the goal of spirituality.

James Hollis refers to this as "the encounter with the reality and magnitude of our own souls." He adds, "That kind of dialogue [as a result of the encounter] is not about withdrawing from the world."[28] According to Hollis, "the numinous"—God—"is something that solicits [our] response." It is "found wherever we are moved and touched—somehow activated psychically."[29] Philip

23. Braxton, "Religion," 4.

24. Oakes, *Theology*, 5.

25. Shapiro, "Roadside Assistance," Spirituality and Health 22:5 (2019) 14.

26. Lohfink, *Between*, 3.

27. Shapiro, "Roadside Assistance," *Spirituality and Health* 25:6 (2022) 9.

28. Kiesling, "Personal Accountability," 48.

29. Kiesling, "Personal Accountability," 51.

Sheldrake states, "spirituality . . . is a process, a movement. . . . [I]t underlines that all Christian spiritual wisdom traditions place an emphasis on growth, development, and transformation. . . . [T]o engage with spirituality is to commit oneself to an intentional and often challenging practice of life."[30] According to Paul Sutherland, "Education is the groundwork that causes transformation."[31] He adds, "Education that is for transformation and not just entertainment requires practice. It takes work and commitment and can be challenging. Education requires us to let go of naïve beliefs, to explore, to inquire, to question everything, to be humble and innocent, but mostly to do the scariest thing we can do: Change."[32] Transformation from change, according to Sutherland, is not a destination "that we arrive at when we can suddenly quit our practice."[33] Our true selves, according to Shapiro, "is pure awareness without boundaries of any kind."[34] Braxton explains: "The self is not an essence, but rather a process that is constantly being updated. . . . [I]t is that feature of human awareness we most associate with ourselves and likely enjoy."[35] Shapiro adds, "The aim of spiritual practice is to undermine attachment to all systems and to prime the pump of awakening that is, in the end, a matter of grace rather than grit."[36] Then, the true self "is free from labels. . . . Once you know you are free from all labels, you can wear any label you want without falling into the trap of identifying with it."[37] With awareness comes enlightenment, which according to Sutherland, "is about wholeness—an engaged connection that simultaneously radiates physical, emotional, intellectual, and spiritual oneness."[38]

---

30. Sheldrake, *Spiritual Way*, 141.

31. Sutherland, "Heart," *Spirituality and Health* 25: 6 (2022) 74.

32. Sutherland, "Heart," *Spirituality and Health* 25: 6 (2022) 74.

33. Sutherland, "Heart," *Spirituality and Health* 25: 6 (2022) 75.

34. Shapiro, "Roadside Assistance," *Spirituality and Health* 25:6 (2022) 9.

35. Braxton, "Religion," 7.

36. Shapiro, "Roadside Assistance," *Spirituality and Health* 25:6 (2022) 8.

37. Shapiro, "Roadside Assistance," *Spirituality and Health* 25:6 (2022) 9.

38. Sutherland, "Heart," *Spirituality and Health* 25: 6 (2022) 75.

Anderson, referencing Michael Singer's *Living Untethered*, states, ". . . [S]piritual growth is about noticing day by day and moment by moment, where we're blocked and releasing those blocks so that the energies of our true self can flow."[39] Sutherland concurs, writing, ". . . [T]he goal of mindfulness . . . meditation, or simple contemplative prayer, is a quiet mind that gets beyond judgment and quits labeling everything in our life as god-bad-neutral. Just seeing life and life's events as they are and then deciding how to respond to them with mindfulness and calm. Our response to an event—and not how we label it—is what we must focus on."[40]

Howard Rice says, "Spirituality is the pattern by which we shape our lives in response to our experience of God as a very real presence in and around us."[41] First, we experience God, consciously or unconsciously. Spirituality is being in harmony with the universe and everyone and everything in it. Once we are aware—consciously or unconsciously (intuition)—we nourish that connection in the way or ways that fill us the best. For some people, Bible reading, Bible study, other study, pottery making, dance, volunteering, cooking, caring for a pet, singing, sewing, etc. is both an experience of God (spirituality) and a means of nourishing personal spirituality. Divine Spirit and human spirit connect. To illustrate this point, Shapiro narrates a parable from the Zohar, the bible of Jewish mysticism: "There was once a cave-dwelling ascetic who ate nothing but raw wheat. Curious about life outside his cave, he visited a city and tasted thick black bread, cake, and honey-dipped pastry. 'What are these made of?' he asked. 'Wheat flour' he was told. 'Then I am master of all of them,' he scoffed, 'for I eat the essence of them all—wheat.'"[42] Then, Shapiro explains: "Commenting on the parable, the Zohar says, 'This ascetic was a fool; focusing solely on the essence, he never learned to enjoy the delights that flow from it.'"[43]

39. Anderson, "Soul," 10–11.

40. Sutherland, "Heart," *Spirituality and Health* 25: 4 (2022) 75.

41. Maher, "Soul and Spirit," 10.

42. Shapiro, "Roadside Assistance," *Spirituality and Health* 25:2 (2022) 11.

43. Shapiro, "Roadside Assistance," *Spirituality and Health* 25:2 (2022) 11.

Knowing the essence, knowing the Divine, is knowing the universe and everyone and everything in it. If all is in God, then all is filled with God, and all can nourish spirituality. We pattern our lives on such sublime experiences that are brought to us by way of the ordinary. Then, we delight in them. The historical Jesus called such experiences the delight of God's kingdom, reign, empire, etc. Being in harmony with the universe is disrupted by chaos. Chaos, the daily pull to disorder or non-patterned life, keeps us out of harmony. Each person must discover and use what works for him or her to bring him or her out of chaos and back to harmony with himself or herself and with all that exists. Commonly called prayer, the practice is to reunite the broken pieces of life into a harmonious whole through reading, study, gardening, walking, painting. etc. Philip Goldberg writes, "Exquisite architecture can evoke awe and transcendence every bit as much as a mountain range or a field of wildflowers."[44] He writes about feeling the energy in "a library especially if you value books . . . . 'Libraries are like mountains or meadows or creeks: sacred space.' A park bench can be sacred space. So can a puddle-sized pond, a pier, an empty ball field, a quiet museum gallery, an unused room in an office building, a hospital chapel, or a lonesome tree. . . ."[45] Goldberg states: ". . . Divine Presence is everywhere, but it is, to most of us mortals, more discernable in some places than in others. . . . [T]he Divine will reveal itself in surprising places, even in a kitchen . . . ."[46]

While saying words—what most people think prayer is—is important, those who practice spirituality know more is needed to transform chaos into harmony. The transformation is done by God to whom we connect through all else. Because we exist in the very One—no matter what name we give—all is done in the divine presence, and we are transformed in the process. We engage in this process over and over and over again throughout our lives, hopefully to finish on the other side of death basking in the divine presence as a transformed self. It makes no difference when we

44. Goldberg, "Holy Places," 24.

45. Goldberg, "Holy Places," 24.

46. Goldberg, "Holy Places," 24–25.

awaken to the divine presence in whom we live and more and have our being. Transformation occurs because we cooperate with God, whether we are aware of it or not. God transforms us over and over again into the divine. And we are not alone in this ongoing process. Shapiro emphasizes that "spirituality is progressive" and, thus, he speaks "of a maturing rather than a mature spirituality. . . . The individual person journeys to the self where he or she knows all is God."[47] Philip Sheldrake says, ". . . [S]pirituality involves a process of transformation that seeks to enable us to move from less adequate values and ways of life to what is more adequate and, indeed, fulfilling in an ultimate sense."[48] Marianne Williamson states, "God works through each of us to the extent to which we make ourselves receptive."[49] All human experience is spiritual, no matter how one limits it with descriptive adjectives, like civil, awesome, secular, religious, etc. Even though we may feel alone, we are not. We are in God. According to Shapiro, spirituality is "a progressive stripping away of the conditioning that blinds [us] to the truest fact of [our] existence: [we] are a happening of God, YHVH, . . . the Happening happening as all happening."[50] Thomas Cathcart, quoting Ken Wilber, states, "A mystic is not one who sees God as an object, but one who is immersed in God as an atmosphere."[51]

Shapiro states, ". . . Jesus was a Jewish mystic who came to know what all mystics know, namely, that all things are a part of God and nothing is apart from God."[52] Michael Casey writes, ". . . [O]ur world is in constant communication with the spiritual world and with God, who stands at its center."[53] This leads Thomas Hubl to state, ". . . [N]othing is not spiritual."[54] Likewise, Rohr states: "I know myself and all others to be a part of God. . . . And

---

47. Shapiro, "Roadside Assistance: Holy Land," 47.

48. Sheldrake, *Spiritual Way*, xi.

49. Kiesling, "New American," 67.

50. Shapiro, "Roadside Assistance: Holy Land," 47.

51. Cathcart, *There is no God*, 43–44.

52. Shapiro, "Roadside Assistance: Holy Land," 48.

53. Casey, *Balaam's Donkey*, 325.

54. Hubl, "Lean."

with this sense of wholeness comes a sense of holiness, a sense of love from and for all beings."[55] Mariann Williamson explains, "Mature spirituality extends beyond the confines of the narrow self. . . . It's a global and universal phenomenon. . . . But you can't ever evolve beyond a connection to God himself."[56] Commenting on the word *namaste,* which means "I honor the divinity with you," Philip Goldberg writes, "It's an everyday acknowledgment that we all share the same divine essence at the core of our being . . . . In short, my essential nature is infinite, eternal Spirit, and so is yours, and so is everyone else's. . . . [W]e are one another."[57] According to Sheldrake, "Christian spiritual traditions all embody a sense of transcendence . . . and point toward a final eternal endpoint for human existence."[58]

While the movement of spirit is different for different people, "spiritual things need physical counterparts to convey their message."[59] In other words, spirituality is the "lived experience of contemporary mystics,"[60] us! And because "we are always beginning the spiritual life, [b]eginning again is about letting ourselves be surprised by God and encountering the familiar with holy wonder."[61] Carl McColman says, "We search for the divine, only to be found by God."[62] He adds, "[T]he God we seek is already present with us, right here and right now. . . . We do not need to go anywhere to get closer to God, for God is closer to us than we are to ourselves."[63] However, spiritual practices awaken us to the divine presence. Sheldrake explains: "Spiritual practices . . . are regular, disciplined activities that both express a particular vision of life and seek to consolidate this through a framework of

55. Rohr, "A Big Experiment."

56. Kiesling, "New American," 64.

57. Goldberg, "Namaste," 13.

58. Sheldrake, *Spiritual Way,* xi.

59. Rohr, "Liminal Time," 5.

60. Rohr, "Big Experiment."

61. Paintner, *Soul,* 98, 106.

62. McColman, *Answering,* 19

63. McColman, *Answering,* 43–44.

meditative action."[64] Rohr states, "Disciplined practice is essential to the spiritual life; yet spiritual attainment is not the result of one's own efforts, but the result of the experience of oneness with Ultimate Reality."[65] Rohr cautions, "We are conditioned to treat the spiritual life as another commodity, rather than as a discipline of inner transformation with a corresponding commitment to alleviating suffering in the world."[66] The individual person journeys to the self where he or she knows all is God.[67] According to Williamson, "God works through each of us to the extent to which we make ourselves receptive."[68]

STOP/MEDITATE/JOURNAL

1. What definition of spirituality above got most of your attention? Why?

2. What is your definition of spirituality?

3. What more do you need to think about after reading the section above?

64. Sheldrake, *Spiritual Way*, 149.

65. Rohr, "Big Experiment."

66. Rohr, "Engaged Love."

67. Shapiro, "Roadside Assistance: Holy Land" 47.

68. Kiesling, "New American," 67.

Title: *A Handbook for Those Who Live Alone*

The subtitle of this book states that it is a handbook, that is, a reference book that gives concise information on spirituality for those who live alone, such as hermits, eremites, anchorites, widows, widowers, young men, young women, solitaries, etc. In general, this book is meant for those who freely choose and like to live alone, yet hunger for spirituality.

Prayer

We make ourselves receptive to the God in whom we live and have our existence through the disciplined activity or practice of prayer. While many people use the words *prayer* and *meditation* interchangeably, Eugene Boylan writes, ". . . [M]editation is only 'thinking about God,' while prayer is 'talking to God.'"[69] He states, ". . . [P]rayer seems . . . to be the result of a progressive intimacy and friendship with God."[70] McColman states, "The contemplative call is a call to intimacy with God."[71] However, McColman considers the use of the word *contemplation* to "refer to silent prayer, centering prayer, meditative prayer, and the prayer of the heart, etc."[72] For McColman, "the heart of the contemplative call [is] the possibility to behold, as an ever-present invitation from the divine mystery. But such beholding is not a task for us to complete; it is a natural state for us to remember."[73] For McColman, beholding "involves gazing, loving, receiving love, a sense of mutuality. We behold God in response to God beholding us. In our beholding, we are transformed."[74] Boylan summarizes this when he writes, ". . . [P]rayer is a supernatural act, and is, therefore, completely

---

69. Boylan, *Difficulties*, 17.

70. Boylan, *Difficulties*, xxxvii.

71. McColman, *Answering*, 27.

72. McColman, *Answering*, xiv.

73. McColman, *Answering*, 39.

74. McColman, *Answering*, 97, 99.

dependent on the grace of God."[75] In the chapters that follow, we will look at ways to pray, prayers to say, and celebrations that may help guide us into contemplation.

Another disciplined activity or practice of prayer is creativity. Rohr states "that each of [us] has the capacity to offer something new to the world."[76] He writes, "A miraculous event unfolds when we throw the lead of our personal story into the transformative flames of creativity."[77] The steps of this spiritual practice, "this creative alchemy," begin by "first get[ting] still enough to hear what wants to be expressed through us, and then . . . step[ping] out of the way and let[ting] it. . . . Such a space is sacred."[78] In the sacred space of creativity, the "divine core of personality which cannot be separated from God" is revealed. Our supreme purpose in life," writes Rohr, "is . . . to discover this spark of the divine that is in our hearts. . . . [T]he divinity within ourselves is one and the same in all." Recognizing the "unbroken awareness of the presence of God in all creatures" leads us to creativity.[79] Thus, "[w]hen we allow ourselves to be a conduit for creative energy, we experience direct apprehension of that energy. We become a channel for grace. To make art is to make love with the sacred. . . . Artistic self-expression necessitates periods of quietude in which it appears that nothing is happening. . . . We have to incubate inspiration. Art begins with receptivity."[80] According to Rohr: ". . . [W]e can't manage, maneuver, or manipulate spiritual energy. It is a matter of letting go and receiving what is given freely."[81]

Mark Nepo accurately summarizes this practice, writing: "By trying to create, we are created. By trying to express, we are expressed. By trying to discover meaning, we become meaningful. So, the measure of great art can be understood, not so much by

75. Boylan, *Difficulties*, 39.

76. Rohr, "Fallow Time."

77. Rohr, "Fallow Time."

78. Rohr, "Fallow Time."

79. Rohr, "An Uncreated Spark."

80. Rohr, "Fallow Time."

81. Rohr, "DNA."

the beauty achieved in birthing a singular piece, but more by the transformation it births in us for the journey of creating it. It is not the thing created that renews us, but the creative act that restores us to our place in the Mystery."[82] Thus, according to Nepo, "Over a lifetime, we experience an evolving sense of fitting things together, through which we are put together."[83] Rohr refers to this as looking at an object and suspending all other activity, being simply aware: "We relax into our basic awareness. We rest with the world as it is . . . . We are face to face with the calm . . . . We contemplate the object as it is. Great art has this power, this power to grab your attention and suspend it; we stare, sometimes awestruck, sometimes silent . . . ."[84] We are one with the created object and, consequently, transformed by the disciplined practice required by the journey to get to such glorious unity.

A third disciplined activity or practice is walking. Erling Kagge says it is essential to human well-being. "You live longer," he states. "Your memory sharpens. Your blood pressure falls. Your immune system gets stronger."[85] While walking may be a slow undertaking, Kagge says, it is a radical thing to do, and, echoing the topic of creativity being a disciplined activity, he states, "[W]alking is a great tool for creativity."[86] Why? Because walking is a spiritual experience, according to Kagge. It is "a spiritual journey. You move your body, and you are being moved. People walk on pilgrimages—no one drives. . . . You can see the world, your fellow citizens, and yourself from a different angle."[87] Walking, as a spiritual discipline, is one of the building blocks employed today to erect Christian spirituality from the bottom-up. Mary DeTurris Poust calls walking an everyday moment, a pilgrim moment. It is "a path that can show [one] new ways to grow closer to Christ."[88]

82. Nepo, "Our Walk," 82.

83. Nepo, "Our Walk," 83.

84. Rohr, "Practice: Contemplating Art."

85. Tassi, "Five Questions," 88.

86. Tassi, "Five Questions," 88.

87. Tassi, "Five Questions," 88.

88. Poust, *Everyday Divine*, 160.

STOP/MEDITATE/JOURNAL

1. When have you experienced God beholding you in prayer? Explain.

2. Among the disciplined practices mentioned above—prayer, creativity, and walking—which best raises your awareness of being in the divine? Explain.

Using This Book

This book is designed to be used by individuals for private prayer and celebration. The goal of this book is to foster the spirituality of the solitary as it flows from the Bible. Chapter 1 presents prayers for the solitary. Chapter 2 is focused on solitary celebrations. A summary is found in Chapter 3.

An eight-part exercise is offered for the sixteen celebrations in Chapter 2.

1. **Title**: A short title is given to the entry. Not only does the title give focus to the entry, but it imitates *Lectio Divina* (Divine Reading), the practice of reading a biblical passage and choosing a word or two from it for reflection, meditation, and prayer, as explained in Chapter 1 and Chapter 2.

   The title is designed to promote mindfulness. According to Annemarie Scobey: "Mindfulness is the practice of maintaining a moment-by-moment awareness of thoughts, feelings, the body, and the surrounding environment. A person who tries to be mindful focuses on what he or she senses and feels in the present moment rather than thinking about what might need to be done later or returning to a memory. Mindfulness is the opposite of multitasking. Mindfulness is truly listening, fully tasting, deeply experiencing; it's taking our feelings as they come and not burying them or pushing them away."[89]

2. **Introduction**: Each celebration begins with an introduction, which gives biblical background to the reader concerning the specific celebration.

3. **Read**: This part is designed to get the reader into the Bible. A specific passage that enhances the celebration is given.

4. **Scripture**: Since the focus of the entry is found in the title, a verse or two from a Scripture passage illustrating the theme of the celebration is presented.

   While reading the biblical text, a word may get the reader's attention. In this case, the reader should follow the guidance of the Holy Spirit and use his or her word for the *Lectio Divina* process of reading, reflecting, journaling/meditating, and praying or contemplating.

5. **Reflection**: The Scripture passage is followed by a reflection on the biblical passage and its application to the theme of the celebration. Throughout the reflections, the masculine pronoun for God, LORD, LORD God, etc. is used. The author is well aware that God is neither male nor female, but in order to avoid the repetition of nouns over and over again, he employs male pronouns, as they are also used in most biblical translations.

6. **Psalm Response**: A part of a biblical psalm is chosen to serve as a response to the reflection. Something in the psalm may spark prayer. All Psalm responses are taken from the New Revised Standard Version of the Bible.

89. Scobey, "Keep Prayer in Mind," 43.

7. **Meditation/Journal**: The Psalm response is followed by questions for personal meditation and/or journaling. The questions function as a guide for personal appropriation of the spiritual celebration, thus leading the reader into personal prayer and/or journaling. The meditation/journal questions are designed to foster a process of actively applying the reflection to one's life and further development of it. The question gets one started; where the meditation/journal goes cannot be predetermined. It may be a single statement or an idea with which one lingers for a few minutes, a few hours, or a few days. Such contemplation has no end; the reader decides when he or she has finished his or her exploration because he or she needs to attend to other things. People who like to journal—written or electronic—will find the questions appropriate for that activity.

   According to Scobey, "Meditation involves quieting the mind and heart."[90] We focus attention on a sacred word, a phrase, or on our breath; meditation is a time of letting our thoughts pass by, without holding onto them or entering into them. It is a time of deep awareness of divine presence in silence and stillness. Contemplation, a cousin of meditation, is resting in God, experiencing God's actual presence, being aware of being in God, experiencing God.

8. **Prayer:** A prayer concludes the celebration. The solitary may use the prayer presented or compose his or her own in response to the spiritual awakening that has occurred for the solitary.

Through this process of prayer with the focus on spirituality for the solitary, the reader will come to a deeper knowledge of and a closer relationship with God.

Notes on the Bible

The Bible is divided into two parts: The Hebrew Bible (Old Testament) and the Christian Bible (New Testament). The Hebrew Bible

90. Scobey, "Keep Prayer in Mind," 43.

consists of thirty-nine named books accepted by Jews and Protestants as Holy Scripture. The Old Testament also contains those thirty-nine books plus seven to fifteen more named books or parts of books called the Apocrypha or the Deuterocanonical Books; the Old Testament is accepted by Catholics and several other Christian denominations as Holy Scripture. The Christian Bible, consisting of twenty-seven named books, is also called the New Testament; it is accepted by Christians as Holy Scripture. Thus, in this work:

—**Hebrew Bible (Old Testament)**, abbreviated **HB (OT)**, indicates that a book is found both in the Hebrew Bible and the Old Testament;

—**Old Testament (Apocrypha)**, abbreviated **OT (A)**, indicates that a book is found only in the Old Testament Apocrypha and not in the Hebrew Bible;

—and **Christian Bible (New Testament)**, abbreviated **CB (NT)**, indicates that a book is found only in the Christian Bible or New Testament.

In notating biblical texts, the first number refers to the chapter in the book, and the second number (following the colon) refers to the verse within the chapter. Thus, HB (OT) Isa 7:11 means that the quotation comes from Isaiah, chapter 7, verse 11. OT (A) Sirach 39:30 means that the quotation comes from Sirach, chapter 39, verse 30. CB (NT) Mark 6:2 means that the quotation comes from Mark's Gospel, chapter 6, verse 2. When more than one sentence appears in a verse, the letters a, b, c, etc. indicate the sentence being referenced in the verse. Thus, HB (OT) 2 Kgs 1:6a means that the quotation comes from the Second Book of Kings, chapter 1, verse 6, sentence 1. Also, poetry, such as the Psalms and sections of Judith, Proverbs, and Isaiah, may be noted using the letters a, b, c, etc. to indicate the lines being used. Thus, Psalm 16:4a refers to the first line of verse 4 of Psalm 16; there are two more lines of verse 4: b and c.

Because there may be a difference in the verse numbers between the New Revised Standard Version (NRSV) and the Vulgate (the Latin translation of the Septuagint, such as *The New American Bible Revised Edition* [NABRE]), alternative verse numbers appear in parentheses or brackets as necessary. This is true particularly with the Psalms, but with other books as well. Thus, NRSV Isaiah 9:2–7 is NABRE (Vulgate) Isaiah 9:1–6; NRSV Isaiah 9:2–4, 6–7 is NABRE (Vulgate) Isaiah 9:1–3, 5–6. Introductory material to Bibles usually indicates which verse-numbering is being used.

In the HB (OT) and the OT (A), the reader often sees LORD (note all capital letters). Because God's name (Yahweh or YHWH or YHVH, referred to as the Tetragrammaton) is not to be pronounced, the name Adonai (meaning *Lord*) is substituted for Yahweh when a biblical text is read. When a biblical text is translated and printed, LORD (Gen 2:4) is used to alert the reader to what the text actually states: Yahweh. Furthermore, when the biblical author writes Lord Yahweh, printers present Lord GOD (note all capital letters for GOD; Gen 15:2) to avoid the printed ambiguity of LORD LORD. When the reference is to Jesus, the word printed is Lord (note capital L and lower case letters; Luke 11:1). When writing about a lord (note all lower case letters (Matt 18:25) with servants, no capital L is used. In *The Message*, GOD (note all capital letters for GOD) is used in place of LORD.

Bibles

Most Bible readers are not aware that there is no such thing as the original Bible! The fact is: There are Bibles. First, there is the Jewish Bible, often called the Hebrew Bible; its books were collected and completed between 70 and 90 CE based on the Jerusalem canon (collection) in this order: Torah (Genesis, Exodus, Leviticus, Numbers, Deuteronomy), Prophets, and Writings. It is important to note the arrangement of the collected books. Second, there is— for want of a better name—the Christian Hebrew Bible, completed in the fourth century CE, but not defined until after the Reformation. It consists of Torah, Writings, and Prophets. It is important to note the (re)ordering of the collected books. Christianity took the Jewish (Hebrew) Bible and rearranged the order of its books!

The Jerusalem canon, obviously, is the collection of biblical books used in Jerusalem and its environs. A large community of Jews, however, lived in Alexandria, Egypt. To the Jerusalem canon (books in Hebrew and Aramaic) they added books in Greek, the language they spoke; this collection is the Alexandrine canon. They also translated the Jerusalem canon's books from Hebrew and Aramaic into Greek. That translation, containing books and parts of books not in the Jerusalem canon, is called the Septuagint (abbreviated LXX). Later, the Septuagint was translated into Latin; it is known as the Vulgate.

Thus, we have (1) the Hebrew Bible—the Jewish Bible, (2) the Hebrew Bible (Old Testament)—the rearranged books of the Hebrew Bible, and (3) the Christian Bible—twenty-seven books originally written in Greek. The Protestant Bible contains only the books in the Jerusalem canon, but rearranged into the Old Testament, plus the Christian Bible books; the Catholic Bible contains the books in the Alexandrine collection plus the Christian Bible books.

The extra books or parts of books found in the Catholic Bible (and coming from the Alexandrine collection of the Jewish Bible), but not found in a Protestant Bible, are collectively referred to as the Apocrypha or Deuterocanonical Books. They include Tobit, Judith, additions to Esther, Wisdom of Solomon, Sirach (Ecclesiasticus), Baruch, Letter of Jeremiah, Prayer of Azariah (addition to Daniel), Susanna (addition to Daniel), Bel and the Dragon (addition to Daniel), 1 Maccabees, 2 Maccabees, 1 Esdras, Prayer of Manasseh, Psalm 151, 3 Maccabees, 2 Esdras, and 4 Maccabees. Not every Christian group, such as Catholics, accepts all of the books in the Apocrypha as Scripture; for example, out of the four books of Maccabees, Catholics accept only 1 and 2 Maccabees.

Thus, there is no single or original Bible; there are many Bibles; it depends on what books a specific denomination or group (Jews, Christians) accepts as Scripture. The Bible that contains any book that any group accepts as Scripture is *The Access Bible* (updated edition): *New Revised Standard Version with the Apocrypha*, general editors Gail R. O'Day and David Petersen, published in New York by Oxford University Press in 1999 and updated in 2011.

Eugene H. Peterson's *The Message: Catholic/Ecumenical Edition, The Bible in Contemporary Language* (with additional translation by William Griffin) was published in Chicago by ACTA Publications in 2013. *The Message* contains the Apocrypha books of Tobit, Judith, Esther with the Greek additions, 1 and 2 Maccabees, Wisdom of Solomon, Sirach (Ecclesiasticus), Baruch, and Daniel (with some of the additions). This book uses *The Message* for most biblical quotations and *The Access Bible's New Revised Standard Version* (NRSV) for some Psalms and quotations.

Thus, a Bible reader should keep in mind the following: In a Christian Bible, The Old Testament consists of the rearranged books found in the Jewish Bible. Roman Catholics and some others add some books and parts of books to that Old Testament because they were found in the Alexandrine collection. In general, Protestants do not add books to the Old Testament; they follow the Jerusalem collection of books, but rearrange them as noted above. Almost all Christians accept the twenty-seven books of the New Testament; there are a few groups that reject one or another of the books in the collection.

Thus, as you can see, this can become difficult to navigate, especially when someone says, "The Bible says . . . ." The astute Bible reader needs to ask, "Which book in which Bible says that?" There is no such thing as the original Bible. There are Bibles, various libraries of books collected over three thousand years by individuals and groups who declared their collection (canon) to be Scripture.

Presuppositions

The HB (OT) begins as stories passed on by word of mouth from one person to another. Sometime during the oral transmission stage, authors decided to collect the oral stories and write them. A change occurs immediately. One does not tell a story the same way one writes a story. Repetition and correction occur in oral story-telling. Except for future emendations by copyists, single statements by characters and plot structure dominate written stories. Furthermore, in both oral and written story-telling, types or models are employed. In the HB (OT), for example, Joshua and Elijah are types of Moses. In the CB (NT) Elizabeth becomes a type of Hannah, who is herself a type of Sarah. When orally narrating or writing a story, the teller or author consciously creates one character as a type of another in order to make the character and his or her words and actions intelligible to the hearer or reader.

In the CB (NT) the oldest gospel is Mark's account of Jesus' victory. The author of Matthew's Gospel copied and shortened about eighty percent of Mark's material into his book and then added other stories to make the work longer. The author of Luke's Gospel copied and shortened about fifty percent of Mark's material into his orderly account and then added other stories to make the work much longer. The material shared by Matthew and Luke is called Q—from the German word *Quelle*, meaning *Source*—by biblical scholars. Mark's Gospel begins as oral story-telling, lasting for about forty years in that form. An unidentified author, called Mark for the sake of convenience, collects the oral stories, sets a plot, and writes the first gospel around 70 CE. Because Jesus was expected to return soon, no one had thought about recording what he had said and done until Mark came along and realized that he was not returning as quickly as had been thought. About ten years after Mark finished his gospel, Matthew needed to adopt Mark's narrative—originally intended for a peasant Gentile readership—to a Jewish audience. And about twenty years after Mark finished his gospel, Luke needed to adapt Mark's poor Gentile-intended work for a rich, upper class, urban, Gentile readership. The author of John's Gospel did not know the existence of the other three works collectively named synoptic gospels.

Furthermore, gospels were not first intended to be read privately as is done today. They were meant to be heard in a group. The very low rate of literacy in the first century would have never dictated many copies of texts since most people could not read, and their standard practice was to listen to another read the stories to them. Thus, what began as oral story-telling passed on by word of mouth became written story-telling preserved in gospels. A careful reading of Mark's Gospel will reveal the orality still embedded in the text, especially evident in the repetition of words and the organization of stories in three parts. In rewriting Mark, Matthew and Luke remove the last traces of oral story-telling.

STOP/MEDITATE/JOURNAL

1. What are the three parts of the Bible? How is each abbreviated?

2. Which Bible do you use: Protestant, Catholic, Something Else? Explain.

3. When notating a biblical text, to what does the first number refer? the second number? the letters a, b, c, etc.?

4. What is the function of LORD (all capital letters) in a biblical text? the function of GOD in a biblical text?

5. How does a biblical book begin, that is, get started to becoming a book? Explain.

6. Which is the oldest gospel in the CB (NT)? Why is it not first in the CB (NT)?

7. How does the original, intended audience of a biblical book affect the way it is composed? Why is it important to know the original, intended audience before reading a biblical book?

1

Prayer

B ASICALLY, PRAYER IS COMMUNICATION with God or another being. Prayer may be spoken or unspoken. It expresses praise, thanksgiving, confession, or a petition requesting help for the pray-er or someone else. Prayer may consist of standard memorized prayers, like the Lord's Prayer, or spontaneous prayer while one reflects upon some passage of scripture from a world religion, a reflection written by an author reflecting on something, writing the answer to a journal question, or meditating. According to Richard G. Malloy, a person prays "[a]ny way that works." He continues: "Prayer does not have to be fancy or professional. Prayers of petition are the most common form of prayer. There are as many ways of praying as there are people, but some practices have proven themselves over the centuries: . . . the psalms . . . , *lectio divina*, the extraordinarily simple yet demanding disciple of centering prayer . . . . All are sane and tested methods of opening ourselves to God."[1] Gerhard Lohfink writes, "Every prayer . . . is a

---

1. Malloy, "Word," 16.

real encounter with God."[2] He adds, ". . . [I]n every prayer . . . God reveals God's own self, and in every prayer, . . . the one praying responds to this divine self-revelation by calling on the holy [n]ame of God, praising and confessing it."[3] "Ultimately," states Lohfink, "prayer means entering into the conversation among Father, Son, and Holy Spirit . . . ."[4]

Joyce Zimmerman says, ". . . [D]aily, quality personal prayer" is good for the solitary. "As we surrender our personal time to spend time with God in prayer," she writes, "we are also rehearsing the kind of surrender necessary for worship to be effective in bringing us to encounter God and be transformed by that encounter."[5] Malloy agrees. "Prayer is a risk," he writes, "because prayer is transformative. To seriously enter into the practice of prayer is to risk having our desires change. Prayer at its best changes what we want. The sanctifying deifying grace of God makes us want what is best for us and for all the world."[6] Malloy asks, "What does prayer do?" And he answers his own question, writing: "Practiced faithfully, prayer frees us from all that keeps us from becoming what we desire to be; prayer frees us for the work God wants us to do; and prayer frees us to be with the source and goal of our existence, our all-loving God. Prayer gives us the grace and the power to do what we could not do on our own . . . ."[7] Stephanos Alexopoulos and Maxwell E. Johnson explain: ". . . [P]rayer . . . is both anamnetic and eschatological; it looks back to and is inspired by the events of salvation history, and it looks forward to the kingdom of God."[8] Salvation history refers to events portrayed in biblical literature, such as the exodus of the Hebrews from Egypt, Jesus of Nazareth's death, etc. The kingdom of God, which is near according to Jesus, was proclaimed by him in parables and other teaching.

2. Lohfink, *Prayer*, 9.

3. Lohfink, *Prayer*, 9.

4. Lohfink, *Prayer*, 14.

5. Zimmerman, *Worship*, 126.

6. Malloy, "Word," 16.

7. Malloy, "Word," 17.

8. Alexopoulos and Johnson, *Introduction*, 212.

Daily prayer is a discipline that brings about inner transformation. While many people use the words *prayer* and *meditation* interchangeably, Eugene Boylan, already mentioned in the introduction, writes, ". . . [M]editation is only 'thinking about God,' while prayer is 'talking to God.'"[9] He states, ". . . [P]rayer seems . . . to be the result of a progressive intimacy and friendship with God."[10] Also mentioned in the introduction, Carl McColman states, "The contemplative call is a call to intimacy with God."[11] McColman considers the use of the word *contemplation* to "refer to silent prayer, centering prayer, meditative prayer, and the prayer of the heart, etc."[12] For McColman, "the heart of the contemplative call [is] the possibility to behold, as an ever-present invitation from the divine mystery. But such beholding is not a task for us to complete; it is a natural state for us to remember."[13] For McColman, beholding "involves gazing, loving, receiving love, a sense of mutuality. We behold God in response to God beholding us. In our beholding, we are transformed."[14] Boylan summarizes this when he writes, ". . . [P]rayer is a supernatural act, and is, therefore, completely dependent on the grace of God."[15]

Malloy reminds us: "There are unconventional ways of praying . . . . See a movie with Jesus; write someone a letter while in prayer mode; create a dialogue with the Holy Spirit; draw pictures for God. The imagination is the arena wherein we can often most powerfully experience God"[16] This book on spirituality for those who live alone is an unconventional way of praying. There are questions for personal meditation and/or journaling. The question functions as a guide for personal prayer and/or journaling. The meditation/journal questions are designed to foster a

9. Boylan, *Difficulties*, 17.

10. Boylan, *Difficulties*, xxxvii.

11. McColman, *Answering*, 27.

12. McColman, *Answering*, xiv.

13. McColman, *Answering*, 39.

14. McColman, *Answering*, 97, 99.

15. Boylan, *Difficulties*, 39.

16. Malloy, "Word," 17.

process of actively developing one's spirituality. Such contemplation has no end.

According to Annmarie Scobey: "Meditation involves quieting the mind and heart. It is a time of focusing our attention on a sacred word or on our breath; a time of letting our thoughts pass by, without holding onto them or entering into them. It is a time of deep awareness. . . . A common theme . . . is silence and stillness. Contemplation, a cousin of meditation, was explained by St. Gregory the Great in the sixth century as 'resting in God.' St. Gregory went on to explain that in this 'resting,' the mind and heart are not so much seeking God as beginning to experience God's actual presence. The reduction of action and thought, according to St. Gregory, allows the person practicing contemplation to sustain [his or her] consent to God's presence. In other words—without action and thought, less gets in the way of experiencing God."[17]

In *From Contemplation to Action*, I wrote: "Contemplation is a spiritual process involving long, thoughtful, steady, serious, and attentive consideration or observation. It is deep spiritual thought or meditation in order to achieve closer unity with God and to discover and understand God's will for the contemplative. Once a person understands or grasps inspired insights into God's spiritual work, then he or she has discerned God's will. However, the activity draws the person into even deeper contemplation to discover further refinement, deeper perception, and greater connectivity."[18]

The best way to contemplate is in solitude, an advantage the solitary enjoys. Sitting, standing, walking, or kneeling alone in silence fosters stillness within a person that raises his or her awareness of the presence of God. It is in silence that the solitary can listen deeply to his or her life and know the change that leads to transformation of self. While traveling the road of contemplation, the solitary discovers ongoing spiritual transformation.

In *Rosarium Virginis Mariae*, Pope St. John Paul II states, "Listening and mediation are nourished by silence."[19] He continues:

17. Scobey, "Keep Prayer in Mind," 43–44.

18. Boyer, *From Contemplation*, xix.

19. "*Rosarium*," par. 31.

"A discovery of the importance of silence is one of the secrets of practicing contemplation and mediation. One drawback of a society dominated by technology and the mass media is the fact that silence becomes increasingly difficult to achieve."[20] "Just being comfortable with silence is being comfortable with allowing things to be just what they are, which is the basic practice of meditation," according to Mirabi Bush.[21] She adds: "Silence allows [one] to be receptive because [he or she is] not busy talking. Silence allows [a person] to listen deeply and just be."[22] Lohfink writes: ". . . [M]editation arises out of contemplation of the works of God. That contemplation may include many things: nature, humanity; the world, the whole creation, the Torah, the nature of God."[23]

People search diligently for God through all types of practices within and outside all world religions, and they give up in exhaustion when they have not found the divine. God cannot be found; God finds us. That is a fundamental truth of spirituality that has been overwhelmed by our individual quest to be in control of all of life. The truth that God finds us is embraced by those who practice silence, such as monks and nuns in monasteries and convents, hermits and anchorites in wilderness hermitages, and all men and women who choose to live as solitudinarians for all or part of their lives. They know how to be quiet within and without and to hear God's voice in their own thoughts and words, in inspired texts, and in nature surrounding them. Such awareness is known as inspiration; it is spirituality through contemplation. It is often called discernment, seeing clearly what is at first not very clear or obvious, understanding what is not immediately obvious, resulting in accuracy of spiritual perception. Divine discernment is contemplation; it results in insight, inspiration, and an awareness of inner truth. Contemplations, consciousness, or awareness

---

20. "*Rosarium*," par. 31.

21. Petersen, "Working," 62.

22. Petersen, "Working," 62. For more on the importance of silence, see *Shhh! The Sound of Sheer Silence: A Biblical Spirituality that Transforms* by Mark G. Boyer (Eugene, OR: Wipf and Stock, 2019).

23. Lohfink, *Prayer*, 152.

is a spiritual awakening that one is connected to everything and everyone that exists. A person realizes that all is in God; all exists in God. Being (God) shares being with all creation and sets in motion the transformation process.

As noted above, contemplation initiates one into God. A person is absorbed into the dialogue of the Father, the Son, and the Holy Spirit, while gazing in total awareness. Indeed, contemplation involves paradox. God can be found, and God cannot be found. Only in solitary silence going deeper and deeper in contemplation does truth begin to spill out of paradox. "The spiritual life is built on bringing together what seems to be contradictory to or conflicting with conventional or common opinion. The contemplative sees that the duality is not the ruth; unity is the truth. Often, one needs to let go of his or her idea of who God is and let God be whoever he is! When opposites are brought together, that is paradox."[24]

The Matthean Jesus teaches solitary prayer. ". . . [W]henever you pray," begins the *New Revised Standard Version* translation, "go into your room and shut the door and pray to your Father who is in secret" (Matt 6:6). Eugene Peterson's *The Message* captures the meaning of that verse by portraying Jesus saying: "Here's what I want you to do: Find a quiet, secluded place so you won't be tempted to role-play before God. Just be there as simply and honestly as you can manage. The focus will shift from you to God, and you will begin to sense his grace" (Matt 6:6).

As mentioned above, a favorite way to enter contemplation is through the practice of *Lectio Divina* (Divine or Sacred Reading). This spiritual practice begins by choosing a word from a text or prayer for reflection, meditation, and prayer. Traditionally, *Lectio Divina* has four separate steps: read, reflect, journal/meditate, and pray or contemplate. Kelly says that "*Lectio Divina* was first established by St. Benedict in the sixth century and formalized by the Carthusians in the twelfth. It involves four steps: *lectio* (read), *meditatio* (meditation), *oratio* (pray), and *contemplatio*

---

24. Boyer, *From Contemplation*, xxi.

(contemplation).[25] *Lectio Divina*, according to Thornton, "has been practiced monastically for untold centuries and is a profoundly flexible way of *connecting* with a sacred text, being *read* by the text, and then led into quiet compassionate communion."[26]

Lectio Divina promotes mindfulness. As already noted, according to Annemarie Scobey: "Mindfulness is the practice of maintaining a moment-by-moment awareness of thoughts, feelings, the body, and the surrounding environment. A person who tries to be mindful focuses on what he or she senses and feels in the present moment rather than thinking about what might need to be done later or returning to a memory. Mindfulness is the opposite of multitasking. Mindfulness is truly listening, fully tasting, deeply experiencing; it's taking our feelings as they come and not burying them or pushing them away.[27]

The traditional Benedictine practice of *Lectio Divina*, according to Kelly, is "reading the passage [or prayer] slowly four times, each time with a slightly different focus." Then, one waits "for the action of the Holy Spirit to illuminate [one's] mind as [one] ponders the passage [or prayer]."[28] If the solitary is reading a reflection based on a text or prayer, usually the reflection "aims to stimulate thoughts rather than to banish them and sees deep understanding as a way to heighten a personal relationship with God."[29]

Many helps to reflection present a question for journaling and/or personal meditation. The question functions as a guide for personal appropriation of spirituality, thus leading the reader into journaling and/or personal prayer. Journal/meditation questions are designed to foster a process of actively applying the reflection to one's life and further development of it. Kelly says, ". . . [C]ontemplation means making the passage [or prayer one's] own by writing about it in the margins, in [one's] prayer journal . . . ."[30]

---

25. Kelly, "Word," 45.

26. Thornton, "*Lectio Intima*," 36.

27. Scobey, "Keep Prayer in Mind," 43.

28. Kelly, "Word," 46.

29. Kelly, "Word," 46.

30. Kelly, "Word," 46.

"Contemplation is the highest expression of [human] intellectual and spiritual life," Richard Rohr quotes Thomas Merton as saying.[31] "It is spiritual wonder. It is spontaneous awe at the sacredness of life, of being. It is gratitude for life, for awareness, and for being. It is a vivid realization of the fact that life and being in us proceed from an invisible, transcendent, and infinitely abundant Source."[32]

"Every development in contemplation reveals more and more of the mystery of silence and the importance of receptivity over effort, especially in prayer," writes Rohr.[33] Rohr writes, "Silence leads to stillness; stillness leads to surrender."[34] According to Rohr, contemplation occurs when our interior silence turns into the awareness of divine presence, spiritual presence. "Always," he writes, "contemplation requires attentiveness to the Spirit of God."[35] Thus, meditation, according to Rohr is "any act habitually entered into with our whole heart as a way of awakening and sustaining a more interior meditative awareness of the present moment."[36] In his *The Universal Christ*, Rohr writes, "Contemplation is waiting patiently for the gaps to be filled in, and it does not insist on quick closure or easy answers."[37]

True prayer, according to Rohr requires openness of heart, mind, and body. "Those who can keep all three spaces open at the same time will know the Presence they need to know. That's the only prerequisite for true prayer. People who can simply be present will know what they need to know—the Presence that connects everything to everything."[38]

Through the process of *Lectio Divina* prayer, the pray-er will come to a deeper knowledge of and a closer relationship with God. Frank Sheed reminds us, "God is not a problem to be solved,

31. Rohr, "Knowing Our Source."

32. Rohr, "Knowing Our Source."

33. Rohr, "Perceiving Reality."

34. Rohr, "Perceiving Reality."

35. Rohr, "Connecting to the Eternal."

36. Rohr, "Sustaining Awareness."

37. Rohr., *Universal Christ*, 8.

38. Rohr, "Open Heart, Mind, and Body."

not even a solution to be admired, but a reality to be possessed, contemplated, conversed with, loved, enjoyed—this is fullness of living."[39] In the pages that follow, I do not attempt to solve any problems or admire any solutions. I hope to awaken the pray-er to contemplation, conversation, love, and the fullness of divine life.

According to Kelly, "*Lectio Divina* teaches that not only can a text become part of us, any experience in our daily lives might reveal the voice of God if we just learn to listen."[40] As you let this book guide you into deeper experiences of the divine, listen to your thoughts, desires, promptings, etc. Rohr writes, "If something comes toward you with grace and can pass through you and toward others with grace, you can trust it as the voice of God."[41] He adds, "We must listen to what is supporting us. We must listen to what is encouraging us. We must listen to what is urging us. We must listen to what is alive in us."[42] Gerard Manly Hopkins (1844–89), an English poet and Jesuit priest, used poetry to listen to himself and hear God. In his famous "God's Grandeur" poem he states, "The world is charged with the grandeur of God."[43] He explains, "It will flame out, like shining from shook foil."[44] Later in the poem he adds a few words about the fullness of living: "There lives the dearest freshness deep down things."[45]

What follows are various versions of the Lord's Prayer in the singular. When most people learn that prayer, they learn it in the plural. Since solitaries pray alone, the prayer in its multiple versions is presented below in the singular. Following the various versions of the Lord's Prayer in the singular, there are psalms or parts of psalms that already appear in the singular for prayer.

39. Sheed, *Knowing God*, 10.

40. Kelly, "Word," 46.

41. Rohr, *Universal Christ*, 88.

42. Rohr, *Universal Christ*, 88–89.

43. Hopkins, "God's Grandeur."

44. Hopkins, "God's Grandeur."

45. Hopkins, "God's Grandeur."

Prayers in the Singular

The Lord's Prayer

Matt 6:9b–13[46]

My Father[47] in heaven,
Reveal who you are.
Set the world right;
Do what's best—as above, so below.
Keep me alive with three square meals.
Keep me forgiven with you and forgiving others.
Keep me safe from myself and the Devil.
You're in charge!
You can do anything you want!
You're ablaze in beauty!
Yes. Yes. Yes.

Matt 6:9b–13[48]

My Father in heaven,
hallowed be your name.
Your kingdom come.
Your will be done,
on earth as it is in heaven.
Give me this day my daily bread,
And forgive me my debts,
as I also have forgiven my debtors.
And do not bring me to the time of trial,
but rescue me from the evil one.

46. Adapted from Peterson, *Message*, 1595–96.

47. If the word *Father* seems too patriarchal to the reader (pray-er) in this
and the following prayers, *Mother, Friend, Lover,* etc. may be used.

48. Adapted from O'Day and Petersen, *Access Bible*, 1675.

Matthew 6:9b–13[49]

My Father in heaven,
hallowed be your name,
your kingdom come,
your will be done,
on earth as in heaven.
Give me today my daily bread;
And forgive me my debts,
as I forgive my debtors;
and do not subject me to the final test,
but deliver me from the evil one.

Luke 11:2–4[50]

Father,
Reveal who you are.
Set the world right.
Keep me alive with three square meals.
Keep me forgiven with you and forgiving others.
Keep me safe from myself and the Devil.

Luke 11:2–4[51]

Father, hallowed be your name.
Your kingdom come.
Give me each day my daily bread.
And forgive me my sins,
for I myself forgive everyone indebted to me.
And do not bring me to the time of trial.

49. Adapted from Hiesberger, *Catholic Bible*, 1325–26.
50. Adapted from Peterson, *Message*, 1686.
51. Adapted from O'Day and Petersen, *Access Bible*, 1768.

Luke 11:2–4[52]

Father, hallowed be your name,
your kingdom come.
Give me each day my daily bread
and forgive me my sins
for I myself forgive everyone in debt to me,
and do not subject me to the final test.

The Didache 8[53]

My father,
who are in heaven,
hallowed be your name,
your kingdom come,
your will be done,
as in heaven so also upon earth;
give me today my daily bread,
and forgive me my debt as I forgive my debtors,
and lead me not into trial, but deliver me from the evil one,
for yours is the power and the glory forever.

ELLC[54]

My Father in heaven,
Hallowed be your name,
Your kingdom come, your will be done,
on earth as in heaven.

52. Adapted from Hiesberger, *Catholic Bible*, 1440.

53. Adapted from *The Didache*, which is also known as *The Lord's Teaching Through the Twelve Apostles to the Nations*, a brief anonymous early Christian treatise written in Greek, near the end of the first century or the beginning of the second century CE, par. 8.

54. Adapted from the ecumenical, modernized version of the Lord's Prayer released by the English Language Liturgical Consultation (ELLC) in 1988, "Our Father–ELLC," LiturgyTools.net.

Give me today my daily bread.
Forgive me my sins as I forgive those who sin against me.
Save me from the time of trial and deliver me from evil.
For the kingdom, the power, and the glory are yours
Now and forever. Amen.

ICEL[55]

My Father, who art in heaven, hallowed be thy name;
Thy kingdom come; thy will be done, on earth as it is in heaven.
Give me this day my daily bread.
And forgive me my trespasses, as I forgive those who trespass
     against me.
And lead me not into temptation; but deliver me from evil
For the kingdom, the power, and the glory are yours,
Now and forever. Amen.

Some Psalms in the Singular

Psalm 3:1–7[56]

GOD! Look! Enemies past counting!
Enemies sprouting like mushrooms,
Mobs of them all around me; roaring their mockery:
"Hah! No help for him from God!"

But you, GOD, shield me on all sides;
You ground my feet, you lift my head high,
With all my might I shout up to GOD,
His answers thunder from the holy mountain.

55. Adapted from the International Commission on English in the Liturgy's (ICEL) version of the Lord's Prayer prepared for use in the English translation of the Roman Catholic Mass that was released in 1973, "Our Father–ICEL–1973," Liturgy Tools.net.

56. Peterson, *Message*, 843.

I stretch myself out. I sleep.
Then I'm up again—rested, tall, and steady,
Fearless before the enemy mobs
Coming at me from all sides.

Up, GOD! My God, help me!
Slap their faces,
First this cheek, then the other,
Your fist hard in their teeth!

Psalm 4:1–8[57]

When I call, give me answers, God, take my side!
Once, in a tight place, you gave me room;
Now I'm in trouble again; grace me! hear me!

You rabble—how long do I put up with your scorn?
How long will you lust after lies?
How long will you live crazed by illusion?

Look at this: look
Who got picked by GOD!
He listens the split second I call to him.

Complain if you must, but don't lash out;
Keep your mouth shut, and let your heart do the talking
Build your case before God and wait for his verdict.

Why is everyone hungry for more? "More, more," they say.
"More, more."
I have God's more-than-enough,
More joy in one ordinary day

57. Peterson, *Message*, 843–44.

Than they get in all their shopping sprees.
At day's end I'm ready for sound sleep,
For you, GOD, have put my life back together.

Psalm 9:1–4, 9–10, 13–14[58]

I'm thanking you, GOD, from a full heart,
I'm writing the book on your wonders.
I'm whistling, laughing, and jumping for joy;
I'm singing your song, High God.

The day my enemies turned tail and ran,
they stumbled on you and fell on their faces.
You took over and set everything right;
when I needed you, you were there, taking charge.

GOD's a safe-house for the battered,
a sanctuary during bad times.
The moment you arrive, you relax;
you're never sorry you knocked.

Be kind to me, GOD:
I've been kicked around long enough.
Once you've pulled me back from the gates of death,
I'll write the book on Hallelujahs;
On the corner of Main and First
I'll hold a street meeting;
I'll be the song leader; we'll fill the air with salvation songs.

58. Peterson, *Message*, 847–48.

Psalm 13:1–6[59]

Long enough, GOD—
you've ignored me long enough.
I've looked at the back of your head long enough.
Long enough I've carried this ton of trouble,
lived with a stomach full of pain.
Long enough my arrogant enemies
have looked down their noses at me.

Take a good look at me, GOD, my God;
I want to look life in the eye,
So no enemy can get the best of me
or laugh when I fall on my face.

I've thrown myself headlong into your arms—
I'm celebrating your rescue.
I'm singing at the top of my lungs.
I'm so full of answered prayers.

Psalm 16:1–9, 11[60]

Keep me safe, O God,
I've run for dear life to you.
I say to GOD, "Be my Lord!"
Without you, nothing makes sense.

And these God-chosen lives all around—
what splendid friends they make!

Don't just go shopping for a god.
Gods are not for sale.
I swear I'll never treat god-names
like brand-names.

59. Peterson, *Message*, 850–51.
60. Peterson, *Message*, 852–53.

My choice is you, GOD, first and only.
And now I find I'm your choice!
You set me up with a house and yard.
And then you make me your heir!

The wise counsel GOD gives when I'm awake
is confirmed by my sleeping heart.
Day and night I'll stick with GOD;
I've got a good thing going and I'm not letting go.

I'm happy from the inside out,
and from the outside in, I'm firmly formed.

Now you've got my feet on the life path,
all radiant from the shining of your face.
Ever since you took my hand,
I'm on the right way.

Psalm 22:1–2, 4–5, 14–15, 19[61]

God, God . . . my God!
Why did you dump me miles from nowhere?
Doubled up with pain, I call to God all the day long.
No answer. Nothing.
I keep at it all night, tossing and turning.

[I] know you were there for [my] parents;
they cried for your help and you gave it;
they trusted and lived a good life.

I'm a bucket kicked over and spilled,
every joint in my body has been pulled apart.
My heart is a blog of melted wax in my gut.
I'm dry as a bone, my tongue black and swollen.

61. Peterson, *Message*, 859–61.

You, GOD—don't put off my rescue!
Hurry and help me!

Psalm 25:1–3a, 4–5, 20–21[62]

My head is high, GOD, held high;
I'm looking to you, GOD;
No hangdog skulking for me.

I've thrown in my lot with you;
You won't embarrass me, will you?
Or let my enemies get the best of me?

Show me how you work, GOD;
School me in your ways.

Take me by the hand;
Lead me down the path of truth.
You are my Savior, aren't you?

Keep watch over me and keep me out of trouble;
Don't let me down when I run to you.

Use all your skill to put me together;
I wait to see your finished product.

Psalm 27:1, 4–5, 7–9, 11[63]

Light, space, zest—that's GOD!
So, with him on my side I'm fearless,
afraid of no one and nothing.

62. Peterson, *Message*, 862–64.
63. Peterson, *Message*, 864–65.

I'm asking GOD for one thing, only one thing;
To live with him in his house my whole life long.
I'll contemplate his beauty; I'll study at his feet.

That's the only quiet, secure place in a noisy world,
The perfect getaway, far from the buzz of traffic.

Listen, GOD, I'm calling at the top of my lungs:
"Be good to me! Answer me!"
When my heart whispered, "Seek God,"
my whole being replied,
"I'm seeking him!"
Don't hide from me now!

You've always been right there for me;
don't turn your back on me now.
Don't throw me out, don't abandon me;
you've always kept the door open.

Point me down your highway, God;
direct me along a well-lighted street.

Psalm 28:1a, 2, 6–7[64]

Don't turn a deaf ear when I call you, GOD.
I'm letting you know what I need, calling out for help
And lifting my arms toward your inner sanctum.

Blessed be GOD—he heard me praying.
He proved he's on my side;
I've thrown my lot in with him.

Now I'm jumping for joy,
and shouting and singing my thanks to him.

64. Peterson, *Message*, 866.

Psalm 30:1–3, 6–12[65]

I give you all the credit, GOD—
you got me out of that mess,
you didn't let my foes gloat.

GOD, my God, I yelled for help and you put me together.
GOD, you pulled me out of the grave,
gave me another chance at life when I was down-and-out.

When things were going great
I crowed, "I've got it made.
I'm GOD's favorite.
He made me king of the mountain."
Then you looked the other way
and I fell to pieces.

I called out to you, GOD;
I laid my case before you:
"Can you sell me for a profit when I'm dead?
auction me off at a cemetery yard sale?
When I'm 'dust to dust' my songs
and stories of you won't sell.
So listen! And be kind!
Help me out of this!"

You did it: you changed wild lament into whirling dance;
You ripped off my black mourning band
and decked me with wildflowers.
I'm about to burst with song;
I can't keep quiet about you.
GOD, my God,
I can't thank you enough.

65. Peterson, *Message*, 867–68.

Psalm 31:1–3, 5, 9–10, 14–15a, 16[66]

I run to you, GOD; I run for dear life.
Don't let me down!
Take me seriously this time!
Get down on my level and listen,
and please—no procrastination!
Your granite cave a hiding place,
your high cliff aerie a place of safety.

You're my cave to hide in, my cliff to climb.
Be my safe leader, be my true mountain guide.
I've put my life in your hands.
You won't drop me, you'll never let me down.

Be kind to me, GOD—I'm in deep, deep trouble again.
I've cried my eyes out; I feel hollow inside.
My life leaks away, groan by groan;
my years fade out in sighs.
My troubles have worn me out,
turned my bones to powder.

Desperate, I throw myself on you: you are my God!
Hour by hour I place my days in your hand . . . .
Warm me, your servant, with a smile;
save me because you love me.

Psalm 34:1–2, 4, 6[67]

I bless GOD every chance I get;
my lungs expand with his praise.

I live and breathe GOD;
if things aren't going well, hear this and be happy . . . .

66. Peterson, *Message*, 868–70.

67. Peterson, *Message*, 872–73.

GOD met me more than halfway,
he freed me from my anxious fears.

When I was desperate, I called out,
and GOD got me out of a tight spot.

Psalm 39:1, 3, 4–6a, 7, 11–13[68]

I'm determined to watch steps and tongue
so they won't land me in trouble.
My thoughts boiled over;
I spilled my guts.

"Tell me, what's going on, GOD?
How long do I have to live?
Give me the bad news!
You've kept me on pretty short rations;
my life is string too short to be saved.
Oh! [I'm a] puff of air.
Oh! [I'm a] shadow in a campfire.
Oh! [I'm] just spit in the wind."

"What am I doing in the meantime, Lord?
Hoping, that's what I'm doing—hoping
You'll save me . . . .
When you put [me] through fire to purge [me] from [my] sin
[my] dearest idols go up in smoke.
[Am I] also nothing but smoke?"

"Ah, GOD, listen to my prayer, my cry—open your ears.
Don't be callous; just look at these tears of mine.
I'm a stranger here. I don't know my way—
a migrant like my whole family.
Give me a break, cut me some slack
before it's too late and I'm out of here."

68. Peterson, *Message*, 879–80.

Psalm 51:1–12, 14–15[69]

Generous in love—God, give grace!
Huge in mercy—wipe out my bad record.
Scrub away my guilt,
soak out my sins in your laundry.
I know how bad I've been;
my sins are starring me down.

You're the One I've violated, and you've seen
it all, seen the full extent of my evil.
You have all the facts before you;
whatever you decide about me is fair.
I've been out of step with you for a long time,
in the wrong since before I was born.
What you're after is truth from the inside out.
Enter me, then; conceive a new, true life.

Soak me in your laundry and I'll come out clean,
scrub me and I'll have a snow-white life.
Tune me in to foot-tapping songs,
set these once-broken bones to dancing.
Don't look too close for blemishes,
give me a clean bill of health.
God, make a fresh start in me,
shape a Genesis week from the chaos of my life.
Don't throw me out with the trash,
or fail to breath holiness in me.
Bring me back from gray exile,
put a fresh wind in my sails!

Commute my death sentence, God, my salvation God,
and I'll sing anthems to your life-giving ways.
Unbutton my lips, dear God;
I'll let loose with your praise.

69. Peterson, *Message*, 891–92.

Psalm 54:1–2, 6–7a[70]

God, for your sake, help me!
Use your influence to clear me.
Listen, God—I'm desperate.
Don't be too busy to hear me.

I'm ready now to worship, so ready.
I thank you, GOD—you're so good.
You got me out of every scrape . . . .

Psalm 57:1–2, 3b, 7–11[71]

Be good to me, God—and now!
I've run to you for dear life.
I'm hiding out under your wings
until the hurricane blows over.
I call out to High God,
the God who holds me together.
God delivers generous love,
he makes good on his word.

I'm ready, God, so ready,
ready from head to toe.
Ready to sing, ready to raise a tune:
"Wake up, soul!
Wake up, harp! Wake up, lute!
Wake up, your sleepyhead sun!"

I'm thanking you, GOD, out loud in the streets,
singing your praises in town and country.
The deeper your love, the higher it goes;
every cloud is a flag to your faithfulness.

70. Peterson, *Message*, 893–94.
71. Peterson, *Message*, 896–97.

Soar high in the skies, O God!
Cover the whole earth with your glory!

Psalm 61:1–5[72]

God, listen to me shout,
bend an ear to my prayer.
When I'm far from anywhere,
down to my last gasp,
I call out, "Guide me
up High Rock Mountain!"

You've always given me breathing room,
a place to get away from it all.
A lifetime pass to your safe-house,
an open invitation as your guest.
You've always taken me seriously, God,
made me welcome among those who know and love you.

Psalm 63:1–8[73]

God—you're my God!
I can't get enough of you!
I've worked up such hunger and thirst for God,
Traveling across dry and weary deserts.

So here I am . . . , eyes open,
drinking in your strength and glory.
In your generous love I am really living at last!
My lips brim praises like fountains.
I bless you every time I take a breath;
My arms wave like banners of praise to you.

72. Peterson, *Message*, 900.

73. Peterson, *Message*, 901.

I eat my fill of prime rib and gravy;
I smack my lips. It's time to shout praises!
If I'm sleepless at midnight,
I spend the hours in grateful reflection.
Because you've always stood up for me,
I'm free to run and play.
I hold on to you for dear life,
and you hold me steady as a post.

Psalm 64:1[74]

Listen and help, O God.
I'm reduced to a whine
and a whimper, obsessed
with feelings of doomsday.

Psalm 70:1, 4–5[75]

God! Please hurry to my rescue!
GOD, come quickly to my side!

Let those on the hunt for you sing and celebrate.
Let all who love your saving way
say over and over, "God is mighty!"

But I've lost it. I'm wasted.
God—quickly, quickly!
Quick to my side, quick to my rescue!
GOD, don't lose a minute.

74. Peterson, *Message*, 902.
75. Peterson, *Message*, 909–10.

Psalm 71:1–3, 5–6, 8–9, 12, 16–24a[76]

I run for dear life to GOD,
I'll never live to regret it.
Do what you do so well:
get me out of this mess and up on my feet.
Put your ear to the ground and listen,
give me space for salvation.
Be a guest room where I can retreat;
you said your door was always open!
You're my salvation—my vast, granite fortress.

You keep me going when times are tough—
my bedrock, GOD, since my childhood.
I've hung on you from the day of my birth,
the day you took me from the cradle;
I'll never run out of praise.

Just as each day brims with your beauty,
my mouth brims with praise.
But don't turn me out to pasture when I'm old
or put me on the shelf when I can't pull my weight.

God, don't just watch from the sidelines.
Come on! Run to my side!
I come in the power of the Lord GOD,
I post signs marking his right-of-way.

You got me when I was an unformed youth,
God, and taught me everything I know.
Now I'm telling the world your wonders;
I'll keep at it until I'm old and gray.
God, don't walk off and leave me
until I get out the news
of your strong right arm to this world,

76. Peterson, *Message*, 910–11.

news of your power to the world yet to come.
Your famous and righteous ways, O God.
God, you've done it all!
Who is quite like you?
You, who made me stare trouble in the face,
turn me around;
Now let me look life in the face.
I've been to the bottom;
Bring me up, streaming with honors;
turn to me, be tender to me.
And I'll take up the lute and thank you
to the tune of your faithfulness, God.
I'll make music for you on a harp,
Holy One of Israel.
When I open up in song to you,
I let out lungsful of praise,
my rescued life a song.
All day long I'm chanting
about you and your righteous ways.

Psalm 86:1–13, 15–17[77]

Bend an ear, GOD; answer me.
I'm one miserable wretch!
Keep me safe—haven't I lived a good life?
Help your servant—I'm depending on you!
You're my God; have mercy on me.
I count on you from morning to night.
Give your servant a happy life;
I put myself in your hands!
You're well-known as good and forgiving,
bighearted to all who ask for help.
Pay attention, GOD, to my prayer;
bend down and listen to my cry for help.

77. Peterson, *Message*, 926–27.

Every time I'm in trouble I call on you,
confident that you'll answer.

There's no one quite like you among the gods, O Lord,
and nothing to compare with your works.
All the nations you made are on their way,
ready to give honor to you, O Lord,
Ready to put your beauty on display,
parading your greatness,
And the great things you do—
God, you're the one, there's no one but you!

Train me, GOD, to walk straight;
then I'll follow your true path.
Put me together, one heart and mind;
then, undivided, I'll worship in joyful fear.
From the bottom of my heart I thank you, dear Lord;
I've never kept secret what you're up to.
You've always been great toward me—what love!
You snatched me from the brink of disaster!
. . . [Y]ou, O God, are both tender and kind,
not easily angered, immense in love,
and you never, never quit.
So look me in the eye and show kindness,
give your servant the strength to go on,
save you dear, dear child!
Make a show of how much you love me . . . ,
As you, GOD, gently and powerfully
put me back on my feet.

Psalm 88:1–3, 5a, 9b, 13–15[78]

GOD, you're my last chance of the day.
I spend the night on my knees before you.

78. Peterson, *Message*, 927–28.

Put me on your salvation agenda;
take notes on the trouble I'm in.
I've had my fill of trouble . . . .
I'm written off as a lost cause,
one more statistic, a hopeless case.

I call to you, GOD, all day I call.
I wring my hands. I plead for help.

I'm standing my ground, shouting for help,
at my prayers every morning, on my knees each day break.
Why, GOD, do you turn a deaf ear?
Why do you make yourself scarce?
For as long as I remember I've been hurting . . . .

103:1–6, 8–17a, 22[79]

O my soul, bless GOD.
From head to toe. I'll bless his holy name!
O my soul, bless GOD,
Don't forget a single blessing!

He forgives [my] sins—every one.
He heals [my] diseases—every one.
He redeems [me] from hell—saves [my] life!
He crowns [me] with love and mercy—a paradise crown.
He wraps [me] in goodness—beauty eternal.
He renews [my] youth—[I'm] always young in his presence.

GOD makes everything come out right;
he puts victims back on their feet.
GOD is sheer mercy and grace;
not easily angered, he's rich in love.
He doesn't endlessly nag and scold,

79. Peterson, *Message*, 940–41.

30

nor hold grudges forever.
He doesn't treat [me] as [my] sins deserve,
nor pay [me] back in full for [my] wrongs.
As high as heaven is over the earth,
so strong is his love to those who fear him.
And as far as sunrise is from sunset,
he has separated [me] from [my] sins.
As parents feel for their children,
GOD feels for those who fear him.
He knows [me] inside and out,
keeps in mind that [I'm] made of mud.
Men and women don't live very long;
like wildflowers they spring up and blossom,
But a storm snuffs them out just as quickly,
leaving nothing to show they were here.
GOD's love, though, is ever and always,
eternally present to all who fear him . . . .

Bless GOD, all creatures wherever you are—
everything and everyone made by GOD.

And you, O my soul, bless GOD!

Psalm 104:1–25, 27–34, 35bc[80]

O my soul, bless GOD!

GOD, my God, how great you are!
beautifully, gloriously robed,
Dressed up in sunshine,
and all heaven stretched out for your tent.
You built your palace on the ocean deeps,
made a chariot out of clouds and took off on wind-wings.
You commandeered winds as messengers,

80. Peterson, *Message*, 941–42.

appointed fire and flame as ambassadors.
You set earth on a firm foundation
so that nothing can shake it, ever.
You blanketed earth with ocean,
covered the mountains with deep waters;
Then you roared and the water ran away—
your thunder crash put it to flight.
Mountains pushed up, valleys spread out
in the places you assigned them.
You set boundaries between earth and sea;
never again will earth be flooded.
You started the springs and rivers,
sent them flowing among the hills.
All the wild animals now drink their fill,
Wild donkeys quench their thirst.
Along the riverbanks the birds build nests,
ravens make their voices heard.
You water the mountains from your heavenly cisterns;
earth is supplied with plenty of water.
You make grass grow for the livestock,
hay for the animals that plow the ground.

Oh yes, God brings grain from the land,
wine to make people happy.
Their faces glowing with health,
a people well-fed and hearty.
GOD's trees are well-watered—
the Lebanon cedars he planted.
Birds build their nests in those trees;
look—the stork at home in the treetop.
Mountain goats climb about the cliffs;
badgers burrow among the rocks.
The moon keeps track of the seasons,
the sun is in charge of each day.
When it's dark and night takes over,
all the forest creatures come out.

The young lions roar for their prey,
clamoring to God for their supper.
When the sun comes up, they vanish,
lazily stretched out in their dens.
Meanwhile, men and women go out to work,
busy at their jobs until evening.

What a wildly wonderful world, GOD!
You made it all, with Wisdom at your side,
made earth overflow with your wonderful creations.
Oh, look—the deep, wide sea,
brimming with fish past counting,
sardines and sharks and salmon.
All the creatures look expectantly to you
to give them their meals on time.
You come, and they gather around;
you open your hand and they eat from it.
If you turned your back,
they'd die in a minute—
Take back your Spirit and they die,
revert to original mud;
Send out your Spirit and they spring to life—
the whole countryside in bloom and blossom.

The glory of GOD—let it last forever!
Let GOD enjoy his creation!
He takes one look at earth and triggers an earthquake,
points a finger at the mountains, and volcanoes erupt.

Oh, let me sing to GOD all my life long,
sing hymns to my God as long as I live!
Oh, let my song please him;
I'm so pleased to be singing to GOD.

O my soul, bless GOD!

Psalm 111:1–10[81]

Hallelujah!
I give thanks to GOD with everything I've got . . . .
GOD's works are so great, worth
A lifetime of study—endless enjoyment!
Splendor and beauty mark his craft;
His generosity never gives out.
His miracles are his memorial—
This GOD of Grace, this GOD of Love.
He gave good to those who fear him,
He remembered to keep his ancient promise.
He proved to his people that he could do what he said:
Hand them the nations on a platter—a gift!
He manufactures truth and justice;
All his products are guaranteed to last—
Never out-of-date, never obsolete, rust-proof.
All that he makes and does is honest and true.
He paid the ransom for his people.
He ordered his Covenant kept forever.
He's so personal and holy, worthy of our respect.
The good life begins in the fear of GOD—
Do that and you'll know the blessing of GOD.
His Hallelujah lasts forever!

Psalm 130:1–6[82]

Help, GOD—the bottom has fallen out of my life!
Master, hear my cry for help!
Listen hard! Open your ears!
Listen to my cries for mercy.

If you, GOD, kept records on wrongdoings,
who would stand a chance?

81. Peterson, *Message*, 951–52.
82. Peterson, *Message*, 968.

As it turns out, forgiveness is your habit,
and that's why you're worshiped.

I pray to God—my life a prayer—
and wait for what he'll say and do.
My life's on the line before God, my Lord,
waiting and watching till morning,
waiting and watching till morning.

Psalm 131:1–3[83]

GOD, I'm not trying to rule the roost,
I don't want to be king of the mountain.
I haven't meddled where I have no business
or fantasized grandiose plans.

I've kept my feet on the ground,
I've cultivated a quiet heart.
Like a baby content in its mother's arms,
my soul is a baby content.

Wait . . . for GOD. Wait with hope.
Hope now; hope always!

Psalm 139:1–19, 23–24[84]

God, investigate my life;
get all the facts firsthand.
I'm an open book to you;
even from a distance, you know what I'm thinking.
You know when I leave and when I get back;
I'm never out of your sight.
You know everything I'm going to say

83. Peterson, *Message*, 968.
84. Peterson, *Message*, 973–74.

before I start the first sentence.
I look behind me and you're there,
Then up ahead and you're there, too—
Your reassuring presence, coming and going.
This is too much, too wonderful—
I can't take it all in!

Is there anyplace I can go to avoid your Spirit?
to be out of your sight?
If I climb to the sky, you're there!
If I go underground, you're there!
If I flew on morning's wings
to the far western horizon,
You'd find me in a minute—
you're already there waiting!
Then I said to myself, "Oh, he even sees me in the dark!
At night I'm immersed in the light!"
It's a fact: darkness isn't dark to you;
night and day, darkness and light, they're all the same to you.

Oh yes, you shaped me first inside, then out;
you formed me in my mother's womb.
I thank you, High God—you're breathtaking!
Body and soul, I am marvelously made!
I worship in adoration—what a creation!
You know me inside and out,
you know every bone in my body;
You know exactly how I was made, bit by bit,
how I was sculpted from nothing into something.
Like an open book, you watched me grow from conception to birth;
all the stages of my life were spread out before you.
The days of my life all prepared
before I'd even lived one day.

Your thoughts—how rare, how beautiful!

God, I'll never comprehend them!
I couldn't even begin to count them—
any more than I could count the sand of the sea.
Oh, let me rise in the morning and live always with you!
And please, God, do away with wickedness for good!

Investigate my life, O God,
find out everything about me;
Cross-examine and test me,
get a clear picture of what I'm about;
See for yourself whether I've done anything wrong—
then guide me on the road to eternal life.

Psalm 141:1–2, 8–9[85]

GOD, come close. Come quickly!
Open your ears—it's my voice you're hearing!
Treat my prayer as sweet incense rising;
my raised hands are my evening prayers.

But GOD, dear Lord,
I only have eyes for you.
Since I've run for dear life to you,
take good care of me.

85. Peterson, *Message*, 975.

2

Celebrations that Enhance Spirituality

B ECAUSE WE LIVE AND move and have our being in God, celebrations presented below are intended to raise the solitary's awareness of this spirituality. Being awestruck by the sunrise peeking over a hill and feeling emotionally alive or observing your shadow from the moon stretched before or behind you and feeling sparks fly within serves to raise awareness of being in God, connected to all that is—dogs, cats, trees, mountains, streams, sun, moon, earth, grass, home (hermitage), etc. Whatever is woven through or entwined in life, spirit, connects with Spirit, like a cable. And the divine manifests itself in us. As Gregory Boyle states, ". . . [I]ndeed the Lord comes to us disguised as ourselves."[1] Through private celebrations, the solitary recognizes and participates in the divine, something religions have taken away and relegated to the domain of clergy. Every solitary is responsible for his or her own spiritual growth today. Thus, celebrations are key moments for those who are in God, because they are experiences

1. Boyle, *Tattoos*, 60.

of simultaneously finding and being found by God. According to the Acts of the Apostles, God "doesn't play hide-and-seek with us. He's not remote; he's near. We live and move in him, can't get away from him!" (Acts 17:28).

According to Richard Gaillardetz, "If we are to flourish as humans, we need authoritative narratives, transformative practices, inherited wisdom, and exemplary figures—all of which are capable of positively shaping our habits, affections, and imaginations."[2] In the exercises that follow, the authoritative narratives come from the Bible; the transformative practices include prayer in the previous chapter and reflection or meditation or contemplation; inherited wisdom is the result of insight from others which the solitary claims as his or her own; and exemplary figures are those the solitary admires: writers, saints, and biblical characters. While Lohfink refers to "[t]he 'religious' sentiment . . . deeply rooted in human beings,"[3] he means the spirituality of the solitary that exists today. The "free-floating forms" of spirituality, he writes, "all relate to natural elements, to the well-being of the individual ego, to self-discovery, and powers of self-healing. Salvation lies in the self."[4] Bob Hurd echoes Lohfink, writing, "The body is the symbol of human spirit or consciousness expressing itself, and in this expression, actualizing itself for itself and others."[5]

Any solitary celebration is a type of ritual. "A ritual is anything that is done with intention," according to Mara Branscombe.[6] She states: "It can be formulaic or intuitive, elaborate or simple, personal . . . . [A] unique frequency comes alive, instilling whispers of the sacred within us. . . . When we answer the call to connect with something beyond the mundane, we generate access to infinite space" and grace. "The mission is to pour presence, faith, and love into what you do daily. What you feed grows. What you nourish will flourish. . . . To build your own ritual-full life, tune into the

2. Gaillardetz, "Loving," 71.

3. Lohfink, *Between*, 270.

4. Lohfink, *Between*, 270.

5. Hurd, "Rahner and Chauvet," 309.

6. Branscombe, "A Ritual," 38.

activities and places where you naturally feel nourished. . . . This is how we can access deeper states of union with self, our loved ones, and the world. . . . Lean into presence when engaging in what you love . . . ."[7] Solitary ritual makes spiritual practice more meaningful in a U.S. culture focused on the individual, capitalism, and electronics. Paul Joseph Chu refers to popular novelist Andrew Greely, who wrote, "Catholic imagination . . . sees created reality as a 'sacrament,' that is, a revelation of the presence of God."[8] According to Chu, a celebration is "a commitment to the goodness of being," that is, "emphasizes God's presence in the world."[9] Likewise Stefanos Alexopoulos and Maxwell E. Johnson make clear: "It is through the celebration of and participation in the sacraments that the faithful enter into communion with the triune God, where [one] experiences the presence of God."[10] While I avoid the use of the word *sacrament* because of the religious baggage carried by the word, through celebrations, the solitary makes "present the mystery of God through which salvation is communicated to the faithful participant . . . . It is through the celebration of and participation in the mysteries that the faithful [solitary] becomes part of salvation history and [is] include in the Divine Economy and Christ is made present and active in every aspect of [his or her life]."[11] In solitary celebrations, "elements (water, bread and wine, oil, paschal candle, ashes . . .) are recognized as a 'sacramental' mediation of the inscription of God by the Spirit."[12] Hurd explains: ". . . [M]editation means that some reality is rendered present and formative, revealed and efficacious, through another. Mediation . . . entails a distinction between the mediator and what is mediated. . . . [W]hat is mediated . . . evokes an identity, a way of being."[13] Hurd adds, ". . . [L]iterally everything can mediate"

7. Branscombe, "A Ritual," 38–39.

8. Chu, "Expanding," 173.

9. Chu, "Expanding," 173.

10. Alexopoulos and Johnson, *Introduction*, xxv.

11. Alexopoulos and Johnson, *Introduction*, 372.

12. Hurd, "Rahner and Chauvet," 303–4.

13. Hurd, "Rahner and Chauvet," 304.

grace.[14] Grace, which is not a thing, is the action of God sharing himself with all of creation. Quoting Louis-Marie Chauvet, Hurd states that grace is "a self-reception; a receiving of oneself from God as a son or daughter," which "gifted identity is an ongoing task rather than a finished possession."[15] Once we recognize that all is in God, grace becomes the action of God sharing more and more of his being with creation. Hurd states it this way: "We exist by God's gift—already an act of love—but more than that, we exist as invited to communion with God. So creation is from the beginning under the sway of grace."[16] This means that a solitary celebration "is nothing other than God's own self-gift in Christ and the Spirit . . . ."[17] Cara Anthony also quotes Chauvet, writing: "God acts in people's lives in a perfectly free fashion . . . . God is not obliged to use [celebrations] to save them. . . . A person may receive salvation without being a Christian . . . ."[18] Celebrations use things, but those are not empty signs, but as signs "through and in which God freely accomplishes what which is signified, not in a manner that can be presumed upon or manipulated, but in a manner that is truly gracious."[19]

Tying together the concept of mediation and grace given above and quoting from John Colwell, Brett Salkeld records: "That which is mediated . . . is the presence and action of this one who loves in freedom; it is gratuitous; it is grace. . . . It is God's presence and action that is communicated . . . and God cannot be manipulated; he is never at our disposal; he is not capricious, but neither is he subject to necessity; a [celebration] may be the means of his presence, but it is never his prison; he is freely and graciously here, but he is not confined or controllable here or anywhere else. . . . God may give himself but he never gives himself away; he never becomes our possession or property—. . . God and

14. Hurd, "Rahner and Chauvet," 307.

15. Hurd, "Rahner and Chauvet," 314.

16. Hurd, "Rahner and Chauvet," 307.

17. Hurd, "Rahner and Chauvet," 315.

18. Anthony, "The Sacraments," 319.

19. Salkeld, *Transubstantiation*, 209.

God alone is the efficient cause of grace in a [celebration].[20] This is why Mary Ehle, quoting St. Oscar Romero, gives the example of a celebration, writing: ". . . [E]ach carpenter celebrates Mass at his workbench, and each metalworker, each professional, each doctor with his scalpel, the market woman at her stand . . . . How many cabdrivers, I know, listen to this message there in their cabs; you are a priest at the wheel, . . . if you work with honesty, consecrating that taxi of yours to God, bearing a message of peace and love to the passengers who ride in your cab."[21]

Human beings are naturally spiritual. They experience themselves as spirit—something more than physical. Some call it mind, some call it love, some call it soul, some call it consciousness, some call it grace. Because everything and everyone is in God, "nature becomes . . . a true exemplification and instantiation of grace."[22] Natural things, such as water, oil, bread, clothing, hands, trees, words, etc., often serve as parables of grace.[23] They flash the divine presence; they mediate God. Hurd states, ". . . God's self-communication [is] immediately present to the recipient through these very media."[24] Stephen Webb and Alonzo Gaskill further expand the concept of grace. According to them, anything that manifests faith saves—"because it invokes the blessings and grace of God."[25] Furthermore: "If we engage with faith and sincerity, these [celebrations] become vehicles for grace. They are not of themselves salvific. But as manifestations of our trust in God and faith in Christ's redemption, they are purveyors of salvation. . . . I . . . preach grace, grace, grace!"[26] Alice Camille summarizes faith and grace, writing: ". . . [F]aith in Jesus' eyes isn't about group identity or religious systems. It's about knowing divine grace when you receive it."[27]

20. Salkeld, *Transubstantiation*, 210.

21. Ehle, *Anointed*, 17.

22. Oakes, *A Theology*, 5.

23. Oakes, *A Theology*, 9.

24. Hurd, "Rahner and Chauvet," 306.

25. Webb and Gaskill, *Catholic*, 40.

26. Webb and Gaskill, *Catholic*, 40–41.

27. Camille, *Transforming Word: C*, 198.

In summary, solitary celebrations using natural things awaken a person to grace, the presence of God. Celebrations remind the solitary that he or she is in the divine. Celebrations using things do not control God or make God present. They spark awareness of the grace with which God constantly floods the earth. The visible makes the invisible known. For a calendar of possible monthly and yearly celebrations, see *Monthly Entries for the Spiritual but not Religious through the Year: Texts, Reflections, Journal/Meditations, and Prayers for the SBNR.*[28]

What follows are sixteen celebrations using natural elements to awaken the solitary to the presence, grandeur, and grace of God. They are in no particular order.

STOP/MEDITATE/JOURNAL

1. What experiences have you had of simultaneously finding and being found by God?

2. How do you take responsibility for your spiritual growth?

3. In what daily rituals do you engage? How does each make you aware of God's presence?

4. What is your definition of grace?

5. What people or things mediate God's grace to you?

28. Mark G. Boyer. Eugene, OR: Wipf and Stock, 2022.

Water

Introduction: Fill a bowl of water and place it before you, or stand or sit by an ocean, lake, river, or creek. At first, just observe the water in the bowl or listen to the waves of the water in the ocean or lake, or the sound of the water in the river or creek as it splashes and gurgles along.

Read: 2 Kings 5:1–19

Scripture: "[Naaman] went down and immersed himself in the Jordan seven times, following the orders of the Holy Man [Elisha]. His skin was healed [of leprosy]; it was like the skin of a little baby. He was as good as new." (2 Kgs 5:14)

Reflection: Naaman was the king of Aram's army general; this means that he was the enemy of Israel. In fact, he had captured a young Israelite girl in a raiding expedition; she was responsible for setting in motion his trip to see the prophet Elisha, who refuses to leave his house but sends a servant to Naaman to instruct him what to do. At first, Naaman refuses to go to the Jordan River, thinking that Elisha would wave his hand over the leprosy and cure him and that the rivers in his own country are cleaner than the Jordan in Israel. After listening to his servants tell him why he needed to do what the prophet instructed him to do, Naaman goes to the Jordan and immerses himself in it seven times, and he is healed. After attempting to give Elisha a gift for his cure, the prophet refuses to accept anything, and Naaman asks him for a load of dirt, which he can take back to Aram and worship Israel's God. "I now know beyond a shadow of a doubt that there is no God anywhere on earth other than the God of Israel" (2 Kgs 5:15). Because God is considered a territorial LORD, Naaman has to have Israelite soil upon which to worship him. Thus, Naaman, the commander of Israel's enemy forces, is not only instructed by an Israelite prophet how to be cured, but he adopts his enemy's God as his own and carries back soil upon which to worship him! And all this takes place near water.

Water is life. That is why Elisha instructs Naaman to plunge himself into the Jordan River seven times. Seven is a sacred number; it is the sum of three, the number for the heavens, and four, the number for the earth. It signifies totality. ". . . Heaven is united to earth in the river water."[29] When Naaman immerses himself in the water, he drowns himself in life—eternal and earthly. Like Robert Duvall, who baptizes himself in *The Apostle* (1997) to a new identity, Naaman immerses himself into new life in God. He becomes aware that his cure is the result of awareness that he is in Israel's God, who has washed him clean.

Naaman undoubtedly acts "under the inspiration of grace"[30] and seeks God sincerely, even taking a load of Israelite soil with him so he can worship the God of life in his own country. According to the *Catechism of the Catholic Church*, such people like Naaman, who "seek God sincerely and strive to fulfill his will, are saved even if they have not been baptized."[31] The *Catechism* explains: Every person who "seeks the truth and does the will of God in accordance with his [or her] understanding of it, can be saved. It may be supposed that such persons would have desired baptism explicitly if they had known its necessity."[32]

". . . Naaman . . . misses the importance of the Jordan River: Joshua crossed it on dry ground with the priests bearing the ark of the covenant standing in the middle and dividing it; Elijah crossed it by rolling up his mantle and striking it, causing it to divide so he could cross on dry ground; Elisha crossed it on dry

---

29. Boyer, *From Contemplation*, 59.

30. *Catechism*, par. 1281.

31. *Catechism*, par. 1281.

32. *Catechism*, par. 1260.

ground by wielding Elijah's mantle, which caused it to divide. All those crossings of the Jordan are meant to echo the parting and crossing of the Sea of Reeds under the extended hand of Moses."[33] In other words, the Jordan River is filled with divine presence. Because we are in God, "any person, even someone not baptized, can baptize."[34] Baptism can be renewed on a daily basis; this means that the tub, shower, ocean, pond, river, creek swimming pool, etc. offer opportunities for awareness of the divine presence to enhance solitary spirituality.

The word baptism comes from the Greek verb *baptizein*, which means *to plunge* or *to immerse*. Most people think of water baptism as washing away original sin. However, in his letter to the Romans, Paul explains that baptism is about dying to a former life and rising to a new life. "When we went under the water," Paul writes, "we left the old country of sin behind; when we came up out of the water, we entered into the new country of grace—a new life in a new land!" He explains: "That's what baptism into the life of Jesus means. When we are lowered into the water, it is like the burial of Jesus; when we are raised up out of the water, it is like the resurrection of Jesus" (Rom 6:3–4). In the water, we die; from the water, we rise to new life, like Naaman.

The celebration of water, which gives life, is an awareness of being in God, the source of life. Even Jesus was immersed in water (Mark 1:9–11) to demonstrate that he was in God. The sign of water—no matter where it is—reveals the presence of the divine. It is a celebration that enhances one's spirituality.

Psalm Response: "The floods have lifted up, O LORD; / the floods have lifted up their voice; / the floods lift up their roaring. / More majestic than the thunders of mighty waters, / more majestic than the waves of the sea, / majestic on high is the LORD!" (NRSV, Ps 93:3–4)

Meditation/Journal: Where and when has water been the vehicle for you becoming aware of God's presence?

33. Boyer, *From Contemplation*, 59.

34. *Catechism*, par. 903; see pars. 1256, 1284.

Prayer: O God, through this celebration of water, grant that my contemplation may spark deeper awareness of your presence and my existence in you. Pour grace upon me, and grant me an abundance of new life every day I live today, tomorrow, and forever. Amen.

Food and Drink

Introduction: Most people eat three meals every day—breakfast, lunch, and dinner. Some people may combine some of those three meals, such as brunch, or omit one or two of them for various reasons. Other people may reduce the size of meals and add smaller ones throughout the day in order to satisfy health requirements. Food, no matter how often we eat, keeps us alive by feeding the cells of our body. We need food for energy.

Every culture has special foods that are prepared for special occasions alongside ordinary or daily foods that are consumed regularly. For example, in the United States, turkey, sweet potatoes, green bean casserole, and pumpkin or pecan pie are staples for Thanksgiving. For Christmas, ham, mashed potatoes, gravy, and another vegetable and apple pie grace many tables. For Christmas Eve gatherings and New Year's Eve gatherings, cheese, crackers, and wine may be served. In other cultures, beer and pretzels may mark many occasions. In the biblical culture, bread and wine were the staples of life. Thus, no matter what food you eat, it represents your wholeness as a solitary. And the food is a sign of being in the presence of God in whom we live and move and have our existence. Just as the turkey, ham, bread, and wine become us, so in God do we become the divine.

We use food for a special celebration because Jesus celebrated Passover using unleavened bread and wine. In Mark's Gospel, the author narrates: "In the course of their meal, having taken and blessed the bread, [Jesus] broke it and gave it to [the Twelve]. Then, he said, 'Take, this is my body.' Taking the chalice, he gave it to them, thanking God, and they all drank from it. He said, 'This is my blood, God's . . . covenant, poured out for many people'" (Mark 14:22–24). The narrative in Matthew's Gospel is altered (Matt 26:26–28); the Twelve are told to drink the blood "for the forgiveness of sins." Likewise, the narrative in Luke's Gospel (Luke 22:17–20) is altered; the Lukan Jesus instructs his apostles to eat the blessed and broken bread in his memory, and Luke presents Jesus blessing a cup before he blesses and breaks bread and another one after he blesses and breaks bread to drink his blood poured out for them. Another version of Jesus' celebration of Passover is found in Paul's First Letter to the Corinthians (11:23–26); for Paul, eating the bread and drinking the wine is a reenactment of Jesus' death in words and actions. Because of the variant narratives of what Jesus did and meant, according to various CB (NT) authors, we can glean that such a celebration was an act of thanksgiving (eucharist, which can also mean *good grace*) to God. Taking food and blessing it is prayer for the solitary. What Liam Bergin says about the eucharist is also true about other foods used in celebration: "The eucharistic bread and wine are already holy by virtue both of the goodness of God that gives these gifts and by the work of human hands that shapes them."[35] In other words, these elements, just like everything else, exist in God; they are God's gifts which, in celebration, we take and bless from what is his in thanksgiving to him.[36] Alexander Turpin, quoting a friend of his, states, "God is bigger than the Eucharist."[37] Likewise, Brett Salkeld, in writing about "the practice known as spiritual communion," states, "the grace of

---

35. Bergin, "Saving Water," 107.

36. Alexopoulos and Johnson, *Introduction*, 83.

37. Turpin, "Of Pandemics," 336.

Christ is not tied exclusively to the sacrament" of the eucharist.[38] A solitary's celebration using food and drink is designed to awaken him or her to the presence of God, who gives the food—life—to people and creatures.

Read: Exodus 12:1–36

Scripture: "GOD spoke to Moses: Using fine wheat flour but no yeast make bread and cakes mixed with oil and wafers spread with oil. Place them in a basket and carry them . . . to the entrance of the Tent of Meeting . . . . [T]ake one loaf of bread, an oil cake, and wafer from the breadbasket that is in the presence of GOD. Place all of these in the open hands of Aaron and his sons who will wave them before GOD, a Wave-Offering. Then take them from their hands and burn them on the Altar . . . —a pleasing fragrance before GOD, a gift to GOD" (Exod 25:1; 29:2–3, 24–25).

Reflection: In the HB (OT) book of Exodus, God tells Moses about all kinds of things that he wants made. He also tells Moses how he is to ordain his brother, Aaron, and Aaron's sons as priests. The entire ordination ceremony is narrated in Exodus 29:1–41. What concerns us here is the use of food, specifically unleavened bread, unleavened cakes, and unleavened wafers. After reading the account of the exodus in Exodus 12:1–36, we discover the reason for the unleavened bread, cakes, and wafers, namely, "The people grabbed their bread dough before it had risen . . ." (Exod 12:34). However, the ancient Israelites considered leavening—what today we call yeast—to be a form of corruption. When celebrating Passover, God instructed the people "to eat unraised bread for seven days" (Exod 13:6) and when ordaining Aaron and his sons, unleavened bread, cakes, and wafers were used. Any sacred celebration required that no corruption (yeast) be present. Ancient people did not understand what we now know about how bacteria (yeast) worked in dough; they attributed it to evil or corrupt forces, which could not be used to mark a special day or week in honor of God. The prophet Ezekiel tells the returnees from Babylonian exile that they should give "the first of [their] dough [to the priests] in order

---

38. Salkeld, *Transubstantiation*, 233.

that a blessing may rest on [their] house" (NRSV, Ezek 44:30). The prophet's words echo the book of Numbers, which instructs the Israelites, ". . . [W]henever you eat of the bread of the land, you shall present a donation to the LORD. From your first batch of dough you shall present a loaf as a donation . . ." (NRSV, Num 15:19–20).

A celebration using food awakens the solitary to the divine presence. Such awakening gives the solitary the opportunity to thank God for the food and to become aware of the good grace which it manifests. The practice of saying grace before meals—a short prayer of thanksgiving—derives from this understanding.[39] This means that every meal is a potential occasion to recognize the divine presence. Because of the ordinariness of daily meals, special celebrations using food have more potential to awaken the solitary to the awareness that all is in God and graced by God.

Psalm Response: "Bless the LORD, O my soul. / O LORD my God, you are very great. / You . . . bring forth food from the earth, / and wine to gladden the human heart, / oil to make the face shine, / and bread to strengthen the human heart. / O LORD, how manifold are you works! / In wisdom you have made them all, / the earth is full of your creatures. / These all look to you / to give them their food in due season; / when you give to them, they gather it up; / when you open your hand, they are filled with good things" (NRSV, Ps 104:1, 14b–15, 24, 27–28).

Meditation/Journal: What food and drink do you use for the different special occasions you celebrate throughout the year? Make a list of special celebrations using food and drink and identify the food and drink used for each. How does each celebration make you aware of being in the divine presence?

Prayer: All food and drink come from your hands, O God. Hear my prayer of thanksgiving for all the ways you nourish my life spiritually. Grant good things to me all the days of my life, and at its end bring me into the fullness of your presence forever. Amen.

39. For blessings of food and drink, see Mark G. Boyer's *These Thy Gifts: A Collection of Simple Meal Prayers* (Chicago: ACTA, 2009).

Oil

Introduction: We use oil—olive, grape seed, sunflower, etc.—for cooking. Oil is also used in medicines to heal wounds; most medicine chests have several tubes of oil-based products used to anoint scrapes and scratches, rashes, and accidental cuts. Dry skin can be smeared with a variety of oil-based products in plastic bottles with pumps that deliver the ointment onto one's hands. Oil moisturizes; it tightens skin to remove wrinkles; it makes skin pliable. Oil is present in deodorants, perfumes, after shaves, etc. In the ancient world, oil was used to anoint kings and sacred objects. In Greek, the word for *anointed* is *christ*. Most Bible translations do not translate *christ* as *anointed*; they merely present the word *Christ*. Thus, in many sources, Jesus is referred to as the anointed, meaning *chosen by God*, but the translation states Christ, which carries connotations of divinity that are not present in the verb *anointed*. Any use of oil for a solitary is the occasion to become aware of the divine presence.

Read: Genesis 28:10–22

Scripture: "Jacob was up first thing in the morning. He took the stone he had used for his pillow and stood it up as a memorial pillar and poured oil over it. He christened the place Bethel (God's House)" (Gen 28:18–19a).

Reflection: The biblical patriarch Abraham has a son named Isaac, who has two sons: Esau and Jacob. Jacob tricks blind Isaac into bestowing the Abrahamic blessing of the firstborn on him instead of on his elder brother, Esau. Then, Jacob leaves his father's camp to search for a wife. While traveling, he comes to a place after dark and decides to camp there. He takes a stone and uses it as a pillow, when he lies on the ground to sleep. And while he is sleeping, he dreams of a ladder that reaches from the earth to the heavens; he sees God's angels ascending and descending on the ladder. Then, he experiences the presence of God, who promises him what he had promised Abraham: land, multiple descendants, and blessings. In other words, God confirms the promise of blessings that Isaac, Jacob's father, was tricked into giving to Jacob!

The people of the ancient world did not share the same understanding of the cosmos as we do today. Our world picture, that is, our world presupposition, is that the sun is the center of our solar system. Planets rotate around it in an elliptical orbit. Earth is the third planet from our sun, and it is a sphere in shape with one orbiting moon. Ancient people presumed that the earth, a flat plate, sat upon seven pillars. People lived on the earth. Above the earth were the heavens, where the gods and Israel's LORD lived. Below the plate, the underworld, is where the dead lived. Thus, a ladder or stairway connecting earth to the heavens in Jacob's dream was his awareness of God's presence; earth and heaven were connected with a ladder. That is why he set up the stone upon which he had rested his head (the place of dreams), anointed it with oil, and declared it to be God's house. The place on the earth where the divine and human met is declared to be a sacred place by Jacob.

Furthermore, the narrator of the account in the HB (OT) book of Genesis writes that Jacob saw angels of God ascending and descending upon the ladder. An unkind history has turned invisible spirits (angels) into winged humans. The development is easy to understand, as ancient people saw birds with wings fly in the sky and depicted angels as humans with feathered wings climbing up and down the ladder. The word *angel* in Greek means *messenger*. In other words, angel is a code word for God; it is another way to write about the divine presence, which the narrative about Jacob's dream ultimately discloses. During Jacob's dream, God appears— Jacob becomes aware of God's presence—and promises Jacob land, descendants, blessings, and protection.

Likewise, the dream motif—God communicating with biblical people through their dreams—is found throughout the HB (OT) and the CB (NT). The divine reveals his presence through dreams, which ancient people did not understand in the same way as we do today. We may think it logical that Jacob's dream occurs during the dark of night, but that, too, is another motif present in biblical literature. Most people associate God with the light. However, as the singer of Psalm 139 states, "It's a fact: darkness isn't dark to you [, GOD]; / night and day, darkness and light, they're all the same to you" (Ps 139:12). Thus, as Jacob is made aware, God is present in both daylight and darkness.

That is why after he awakens from sleep and he becomes aware of the divine presence, he takes oil and anoints the stone upon which he had laid his head. The act of pouring oil on the stone christened or declared it to be both a memorial of Jacob's experience of God and a sacred place, a place where heaven and earth unite. Likewise, any type of anointing that the solitary may do to a wound—a scrape, scratch, or rash—or dry skin, or the use of deodorants or perfumes, or for cooking is a celebration and an opportunity to become aware of God's presence.

Psalm Response: "The LORD is my shepherd, I shall not want. / He makes me lie down in green pastures; / he leads me beside still waters; / he restores my soul. / He leads me in right paths / for his name's sake. / You prepare a table before me / in the presence of my enemies; / you anoint my head with oil; / my cup overflows. / Surely goodness and mercy shall follow me / all the days of my life, / and I shall dwell in the house of the LORD / my whole life long" (NRSV, Ps 23:1–3, 5–6).

Meditation/Journal: In what sacred place have you encountered the divine presence? Make a list of special celebrations using oil and identify the oil used for each. How does each celebration make you aware of being in the divine presence?

Prayer: God of Jacob, you come from the heavens to encounter people on the earth. Make me aware of your presence whenever I use oil in the light and in the darkness, and grant me the grace to thank you for such grace now and forever. Amen.

Hands

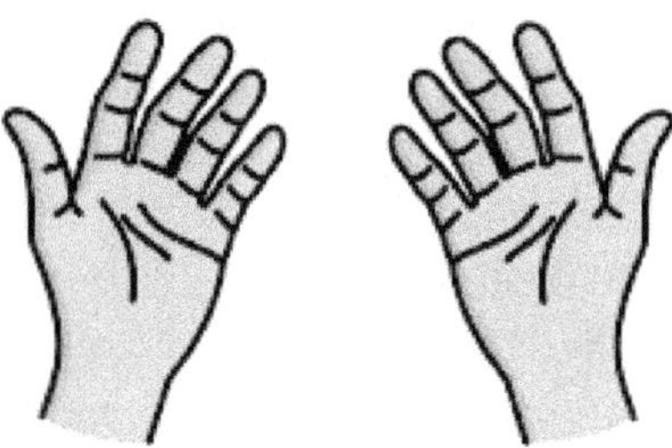

Introduction: Paying attention to the way the solitary uses his or her hands is a celebration of God's presence and an opportunity to enhance spirituality. From the moment we arise in the morning until the time we go to bed in the evening, we are using our hands to wash, dress, prepare food, clean our living space, drive, eat, carry, etc. The hands of another may massage our muscles. The hands of our doctor may examine our body. The hands of a friend may support us. We may use our hands on the head of another to bless him or her or to pet the cat or scratch the dog which lives with us. We use our hands to pay our credit card bills, mortgages, and car payments. Those chosen to lead our world make us aware of the importance of leadership, forgiveness, and awakens us to the divine presence.

Read: Genesis 48:1–22

Scripture: ". . . Jacob noticed Joseph's sons and said, 'Who are these?' Joseph told his father, 'They are my sons whom God gave to me in this place [Egypt].' 'Bring them to me,' he said, 'so I can bless them.' Israel's [Jacob's] eyesight was poor from old age; he was nearly blind. So Joseph brought them up close. Old Israel kissed and embraced them and then said to Joseph, 'I never expected to see your face again, and now God has let me see your children as well.' . . . Then Joseph took the two boys, Ephraim with his right hand setting him to Israel's left, and Manasseh with his left hand setting him to Israel's right, and stood them before him. But Israel crossed his arms and put his right hand on the head of Ephraim who was the younger and his left hand on the head of Manasseh, the firstborn. Then he blessed them . . ." (Gen 48:8–11, 13–15a).

Reflection: According to the biblical story, Jacob—later named Israel—takes his family to Egypt to escape the famine in his own land. Before he gets there, Jacob's sons sell their brother, Joseph, to slavers traveling to Egypt. Joseph rises through the ranks in Egypt and becomes second in command to Pharaoh and is put in charge of preparing for the imminent famine. Jacob thinks that Joseph is dead, and he is surprised to find him occupying such a place of authority in Egypt. As Jacob grows old and blind, he meets Joseph's sons—Ephraim and Manasseh—and he blesses them after recounting his own experience of God at Bethel and the promises that God made to him there. The reader remembers that Jacob had tricked his elder brother, Esau, out of the birthright blessing. The account of Jacob's blessing of Joseph's sons is written to echo that story. Joseph presents Manasseh and places him under Jacob's right hand, and he presents Ephraim and places him under Jacob's left hand. Manasseh is the elder and should receive the blessing, but Jacob crosses his arms and blesses Ephraim instead. When Joseph attempts to correct his father's mistake, Jacob insists on blessing Joseph's younger son. Thus, is re-enacted the event of Jacob, the younger son of Isaac, receiving the blessing that should have been bestowed upon Esau, his older brother. Also, is presented a recurring biblical motif of the younger son receiving what should have been given to the older son to indicate that God doesn't see people the way that people do.

In later biblical writings, the lists of the twelves sons of Jacob will omit Joseph and refer to the half-tribe of Ephraim and the half-tribe of Manasseh. There is never a tribe of Joseph. The laying of Jacob's right hand on Ephraim's head transfers to him the promises made to Abraham, who transferred them to Isaac, who transferred them to Jacob. In other words, Jacob has transferred his leadership authority to Ephraim—not to Manasseh and not to any one of his other eleven sons! With his right hand on Ephraim's head, Jacob has made Joseph and his son aware of the divine presence through blessing.

Besides designating leadership and blessing, hands stretch out over another person can indicate forgiveness. *The Roman Missal* makes clear that "the Spirit himself is the remission of all sins."[40] It also presents a prayer addressed to the Lord Jesus Christ, which asks him to free the pray-er by his "most holy body and blood from all . . . sins . . . ."[41] The laying on of hands by extending them over someone or touching the head of someone indicates "a radical reorientation of [one's] whole life . . . . [I]t entails the desire and resolution to change one's life, with hope in God's mercy and trust in the help of his grace."[42] The *Catechism* makes clear, "Only God forgives sins."[43] Perfect contrition, that is sorrow for sin and the resolution not to sin again, remits all sins.[44] This is true, as Paul writes to the Romans: "By entering through faith into what God has always wanted to do for us—set us right with him, makes us fit for him—we have it all together with God because of our Master Jesus. And that's not all: We throw open our doors to God and discover at the same moment that he has already thrown open his door to us. We find ourselves standing where we always hoped we might stand—out in the wide open spaces of God's grace and glory, standing tall and shouting our praise" (Rom 5:1–2). The act of God setting us right with himself in the translation above is often translated as *justification* or *righteousness*. Quoting Paul Tillich, Edward Oaks states, "[J]ustification means accepting that you are accepted even though you are unacceptable."[45] Celebrating the use of hands makes us aware that we are in the God who stretches out his hands toward us and how we, without his help, are unable

40. *Roman Missal*, 444.

41. *Roman Missal*, 668.

42. *Catechism*, par. 1431.

43. *Catechism*, par. 1441

44. *Catechism*, pars. 1451–52.

45. Oakes, *Theology*, 67.

to reach out to join our hands to his. Because we are in God, God has justified and forgiven us and made us acceptable to himself.

Psalm Response: "[The LORD] reached down from on high, he took me; / he drew me out of mighty waters. / He delivered me from my strong enemy, and from those who hated me; / for they were too mighty for me. / He brought me out into a broad place; / he delivered me, because he delighted in me. / The LORD reward-ed me according to my righteousness; / according to the cleanness of my hands he recompensed me" (NRSV, Ps 18:16–17, 19–20).

Meditation/Journal: Upon whom have you extended your hands in blessing and/or forgiveness? How did you experience being in the divine presence? Who has laid hands upon you? How did he or she make you aware of being in the divine presence?

Prayer: Like a mother, you stretch out your hands toward me, O God, to bless and to forgive me. Draw me closer and closer to you in whom I live and move and have my being today, tomorrow, and forever. Amen.

Incense

Introduction: Incense, a gum or wood that gives off a pleasant smell when burned, uses one's nose to raise awareness that we are in the divine presence. Incense comes in many different forms. For example, there are incense sticks, which once lit with a match on one end and put in a fire-proof vessel, burn and give off a pleasing fragrance all the way to the other end. There exist many different forms of powdered incense, which when sprinkled on small charcoal briquettes, burn and emit smoke that is pleasing to the nose. Incense assists in centering the self and making one aware of being in the divine. According to "Incense as a Timer:" "... [B]urning incense is believed to deepen our attention and empower our spiritual focus. The aroma of incense can help ... tap in[to] ... spiritual connections. It calms the environment and ... mind, cleansing the space for inner and outer journeys."[46] The author of the HB (OT) book of Proverbs states, "Perfume and incense make the heart glad ..." (Prov 27:9a).

In some biblical books, such as Leviticus and Jeremiah, incense is referred to as frankincense. The word *frankincense* is the composite of the Old French *franc*—meaning *noble, pure,* and *high quality*—and *incense* from the Latin *incendere,* meaning *to set on fire; incendere* is based on the Latin *candere,* meaning *to glow.* More specifically, frankincense consists of an aromatic resin obtained from several species of specific trees. Many people have heard of frankincense, because it is mentioned as one of three gifts given to the baby Jesus by "a band of scholars" (often called magi or wise men) in a unique story in Matthew's Gospel (2:1, 11). Incense can be made from gums, resins, wood powders, herbs, flowers, and spices or a combination of fragrant gums, resins, wood powders, herbs, flowers, and spices. Rising smoke recalls the divine presence manifested in the Tent of Meeting and, thereafter, the Jerusalem Temple. And, as we will see below, the smoke represents prayers rising to God.

All that is needed to burn incense is a ceramic bowl filled with sand or small gravel upon which can be placed a lit piece of charcoal or into which can be stuck lit incense sticks. As the powdered incense burns on the charcoal, smoke curls and rises and fills the room with a pleasing aroma. Likewise, as incense sticks burn, smoke rises and spreads a pleasing fragrance throughout the room.

Read: Exodus 30:34–37 and Leviticus 16:11–13

---

46. "Incense."

Scripture: "So I [, John of Patmos,] looked, and there, surrounded by Throne, Animals, and Elders, was a Lamb, slaughtered but standing tall. Seven horns he had, and seven eyes, the Seven Spirits of God sent into all the earth. He came to the One Seated on the Throne and took the scroll from his right hand. The moment he took the scroll, the Four Animals and Twenty-four Elders fell down and worshiped the Lamb. Each had a harp and each had a bowl, a gold bowl filled with incense, the prayers of God's holy people. And they sang a new song . . ." (Rev. 5:6–9a).

Reflection: The CB (NT) book of Revelation is divided into three basic stories. The first takes place on Patmos, the island upon which the author finds himself. The second takes place in heaven, and the third occurs on earth. The passage above comes from the second story in which Jesus is portrayed as a slain Lamb, who is worshiped by Animals and Elders. The author, John of Patmos, is portrayed as a heavenly traveler who is able to enter the door (portal) that opens to heaven, where he gets a glimpse of God's court.

The slaughtered Lamb, of course, represents the crucified Jesus. The fact that the Lamb has seven horns and seven eyes—indicating his perfection (seven is the sum of three, representing the heavens, and four, representing the earth)—as the Seven Spirits of God sent to all the earth indicate that the divine presence is everywhere both in the heavens and on the earth. Thus, God permeates the universe. Because we live on the earth, we live in the divine, who weaves the Spirit into the fiber of our being.

The Lamb takes the scroll, representing the word of God, in his right hand, the hand of power, and the Four Animals, who appeared earlier in the book (Rev 4:6), and the Twenty-four Elders, who also appeared earlier in the book (Rev 4:4), prostrate themselves in worship of the Lamb (Jesus Christ). Each Elder holds a harp in one hand and a gold bowl of burning incense in the other. The author of the book states that the incense represents the prayers of God's people being presented at the divine throne. The burning incense also represents the divine presence, as it did in the portable ark of the covenant and in the Temple. With their harps, the Elders sing a new song, as the Lamb's work (teaching, death, and resurrection) has begun a new age. The lyrics of the new song, which explain what the Lamb has done, are these: "Worthy! Take the scroll, open its seals. / Slain! Paying in blood, you bought men and women, / Bought them back from all over the earth, / Bought them back for God. / Then you made them a Kingdom, Priests for our God, / Priest-kings to rule over the earth" (Rev. 5:9–10).

Later, in the same section of the book, prayers are again signified by incense: ". . . [A]nother Angel, carrying a gold censer, came and stood at the Altar. He was given a great quantity of incense so that he could offer up the prayers of all the holy people of God on the Golden Altar before the Throne. Smoke billowed up from the incense-laced prayers of the holy ones, rose before God from the hand of the Angel" (Rev. 8:3–4). The scenes portrayed in the book of Revelation are echoed in Psalm 141: "GOD, come close. Come quickly! / Open your ears—it's my voice you're hearing! / Treat my prayer as sweet incense rising; / my raised hands are my evening prayers" (Ps 141:1–2).

While Psalm 141 associates the burning of incense with evening prayer, incense or frankincense can be burned at any time to raise one's awareness of being in the divine presence. As the incense burns and smoke fills the room, a person is awakened through eyesight and smell to being in God. Just as the smoke of the incense rises, so are our prayers of petition and praise presented to the divine, while sitting quietly, reading the Bible, or reading a spiritually-enlightening book.

Psalm Response: "I call upon you, O LORD; come quickly to me; / give ear to my voice when I call to you. / Let my prayer be counted as incense before you, / the lifting up of my hands as an evening sacrifice" (NRSV, Ps 141:1–2).

Meditation/Journal: How does incense deepen your attention to being in the divine? How does incense empower your spiritual focus? How does incense make your heart glad? What do you pray while incense burns: petitions, praise, silence?

Prayer: Listen to my prayer, O LORD. See my prayer rising around you, like burning incense. Worthy is your Son, the Lamb, who was slaughtered, to receive power and wealth and wisdom and might and honor and glory and blessing forever and ever. Amen.

Soil (Dirt)

Introduction: A celebration in honor of the soil refers to dirt or dust. Some people make vegetable gardens, flower gardens, fruit arbors, or herb gardens. All of those require good soil in which to grow produce. A friend calls working in the soil "dirt therapy." Many people have a houseplant or two growing in pots filled with potting soil or garden soil. To celebrate soil all that is needed is a house plant placed in one's prayer area or a walk to or in your garden or in a public garden or park. Getting your hands dirty, getting dirt under your finger nails, puts you in touch both with your origins and with your end. Reflecting upon his origin and his end lead the author of the HB (OT) book of Genesis to write in the second story of creation: ". . . God formed Man out of dirt from the ground and blew into his nostrils the breath of life. The Man came alive—a living soul" (Gen 2:7). A few verses later, that same author will portray God saying, "Until you return to that ground yourself, dead and buried; you started out as dirt, you'll end up dirt" (Gen 3:19).

Genesis also tells us, "Noah, a farmer, was the first to plant a vineyard" (Gen 9:20). Likewise, the HB (OT) book of Second Chronicles tells us that King Uzziah "had farmers and vinedressers at work in the hills and fields—he loved growing things" (2 Chr

26:10). A celebration of the soil can take the form of preparing the soil for any kind of garden.

In the narrative concerning Abraham, God is portrayed telling the patriarch, "I'll make your descendants like dust—counting your descendants will be as impossible as counting the dust of the Earth" (Gen 13:16). In his dialogue with God, Abraham refers to himself as "a mere mortal made from a handful of dirt" (Gen 18:27). And to Jacob, Abraham's grandson, God says, "Your descendants will be as the dust of the Earth; they'll stretch from west to east and from north to south" (Gen 28:14). A celebration of soil can be focused on making a list of ancestors, descendants, uncles and aunts, or first, second, and third cousins to become aware of how numerous families become.

Thus, dirt has been raised to a new dignity. Humankind, dust, has been enlivened in God with the divinity's own breath. And Abraham and Jacob are promised that their descendants will be so numerous that they will not be able to be counted; it will be like trying to count the dust of the Earth.

Read: 2 Kgs 5:1–19a

Scripture: "'If you won't take anything,' said Naaman [to Elisha] 'let me ask you for something: Give me a load of dirt, as much as a team of donkeys can carry, because I'm never again going to worship any god other than GOD'" (2 Kgs 5:17).

Reflection: In the story of Elisha, a man of God and a prophet, and Naaman, the commander of the army of the king of Aram, the enemy of Israel, the narrator informs the reader that the great man Naaman has leprosy, any type of skin disease in the ancient world. Naaman's king sends him to the king of Israel for healing. When Elisha hears about that, he tells the king to send Naaman to him. When Naaman arrives at Elisha's door, the prophet will not come out to see his enemy. He tells him to go to the Jordan River and plunge himself into the water seven times and he will be cured of his leprosy. Naaman, however, wanted to see Elisha perform some magic to cure him. The general knows that the rivers in his home country are cleaner than the Jordan. So, he decides not to do as

Elisha told him until he is urged by his servants—who received advice from a slave girl captured in a raid upon Israel—to do so. Naaman's servants prevail, and Naaman takes a dip in the Jordan River, immersing himself seven times. Upon coming out of the water the last time, he realizes that he has been cured of his leprosy.

With his entire entourage he returns to Elisha's front door. This time Elisha stands outside before it listening as Naaman says, "I know now beyond a shadow of a doubt that there is no God anywhere on earth other than the God of Israel. In gratitude let me give you a gift" (2 Kgs 5:15). Elisha refuses to take a gift, because he knows that it was God who healed Naaman; he did not heal him, and, therefore, he could take no gift. Once Naaman is unable to give something to Elisha, he asks Elisha for two mule-loads of earth so that he could worship the LORD (Yahweh) on Israelite soil. Naaman considers the LORD to be an Israelite God who was worshiped only on the dirt in Israel; in other words, Yahweh is a regional god in Naaman's thinking. Elisha quickly expands the idea telling Naaman that he can worship the LORD anywhere, and everything will be OK. Yahweh is the universal God in whom all people and all things live and move and have their existence and life. As Naaman raises soil or dirt or dust to a new dignity, Elisha raises Naaman to a new awareness—Naaman, even though he is Israel's enemy, is in God.

Psalm Response: "Lord, you have been our dwelling place in all generations. / Before the mountains were brought forth, / or ever you had formed the earth and the world, / from everlasting to everlasting you are God. / You turn us back to dust, / and say, 'Turn back, you mortals.' / For a thousand years in your sight / are like yesterday when it is past, / or like a watch in the night" (NRSV, Ps 90:1–4).

Meditation/Journal: What consolation do you receive from knowing that you are dust and you will return to dust one day? Make a list of your extended family members' names, including parents, brothers and sisters, maternal and fraternal grandparents and great grandparents, uncles, aunts, first cousins, second cousins, third cousins, great uncles and great aunts, etc. Identify which ones have returned to dust with a + beside their names. What else do you notice about your list?

Prayer: Creator God, in my mother's womb you formed me from the dust of the earth and breathed into me the spirit of life. Re-awaken the spirit, the imprint of divinity, within me and show me your face. You are one God—Father, Son, and Spirit—forever and ever. Amen.

Oak Tree

Introduction: Even though everyone and everything is in God, some things—in this case the oak tree—became sacred places which raise a person's awareness of being in the divine presence and, thus, enhancing his or her spirituality. Older translations of the Bible referred to oak trees as terebinths. Because oak trees were large with huge canopies, according to the author of the HB (OT) book of Genesis, Abraham thought they were a good place to camp. After passing through Canaan on his inaugural visit, the patriarch "passed through the country as far as Shechem and the Oak of Moreh" (Gen 12:6); the oak tree there was large enough to be named! Shortly thereafter, he "moved his tent. He went and settled by the Oaks of Mamre in Hebron" (Gen 13:18; see 14:13). To recognize the divine presence, Abraham built an altar at both locations (Gen 12:7b, 13:18).

While he is camped at the Oaks of Mamre, "sitting at the entrance of his tent" during "the hottest part of the day" God appears to him (Gen 18:1). In other words, Abraham becomes aware of God's presence with the arrival of three strangers who approach his campsite. Likewise, the oak in Ophrah is the place where "the angel of GOD"—a code name for God—appears to Gideon (Judg 6:11–12). In the shade of the oak tree, the angel of God presents fire, which consumes the offering Gideon presents, before disappearing (Judg 6:19–23). Likewise, Ezra narrates that he "was sitting under an oak," when "suddenly a voice came out of a bush opposite" him and called him by name (2 Esd 14:1). While camped or sitting under an oak tree, Abraham, Gideon, and Ezra became aware that they were in the divine presence.

Oak trees serve as boundary markers (Josh 19:33, 24:26; 1 Sam 10:3) because of their longevity. However, an oak tree is the place of death for Absalom, King David's rebellious son. As Absalom runs from David's army, "riding his mule, . . . the mule ran under the branches of a huge oak tree. Absalom's head was caught in the oak and he was left dangling between heaven and earth, the mule running right out from under him. A solitary soldier saw him and reported it to Joab [, David's army commander], 'I saw Absalom hanging from an oak tree!'" (2 Sam 18:9–10) After this, Joab took three knives and stabbed Absalom in the heart "while he was still alive in the tree" (2 Sam 18:14b). Absalom's dangling between heaven and earth signifies the next scene in the story. Depending upon who finds him caught in the oak tree, he might have life on the earth or life in the heavens. The strength of the oak tree (Amos 2:9; Sir 24:16) becomes Absalom's downfall. In other words, King David is the oak tree, and Absalom is the acorn whose revolt is squelched by his father, and he is left dead at the hand of Joab.[47]

Read: 1 Chronicles 10:1–14

Scripture: "Jacob and his company arrived at . . . Bethel . . . . He built an altar there and named it El-Bethel (God-of-Bethel) because that's where God revealed himself to him when he was

---

47. For more on celebrating trees, especially oak trees, see "Oak" in Mark G. Boyer's *An Abecedarian of Sacred Trees: Spiritual Growth through Reflections on Woody Plants* (Eugene, OR: Wipf and Stock, 2016) 106–11.

running from his brother. And that's when Rebekah's nurse, Deborah, died. She was buried just below Bethel under the oak tree. It was named Allon-Bacuth (Weeping Oak)" (Gen 35:6–8).

Reflection: After he tricks his father, Isaac, into giving him his blessing, Jacob flees his father's camp in order to escape the retribution of his brother, Esau, for having stolen his birthright. God calls Jacob to return to Bethel, where he had the dream of the ladder connecting earth to the heavens. Before he begins the journey, however, he tells his family to remove all the alien gods they have. "Jacob buried them under the oak tree in Shechem" (Gen 35:4). Then, all proceed to Bethel, where Jacob acknowledges the presence of the divine by building an altar (Gen 35:7). In that place, Deborah, nurse of Jacob's mother, Rebekah, died, and she was buried under an oak tree, appropriately named Weeping Oak.

After the Philistines killed King Saul's three sons and he is wounded and commits suicide, the chronicler writes, "All of . . . [the] fighting men [of Jabesh Gilead] went into action—retrieved the bodies of Saul and his sons and brought them to Jabesh, gave them a dignified burial under the oak at Jabesh, and mourned their death for seven days" (1 Chr 10:11–12). Deborah and Saul and his three sons are buried under an oak tree; not only does this reflect an ancient custom of burying the dead below trees, but the oak's longevity provides a marker that lasts a long time identifying the burial site. ". . . [T]he oak tree is a sign of strength, might, endurance, longevity, nobility, courage, and pride. . . . Because the tree has roots that go deep into the earth and boughs that reach high into the heavens, it connects all levels of a three-storied universe. . . ."[48] Thus, from a spiritual point of view, the dead buried under an oak tree remain a part of the earth, even though they are entombed in the underworld while being connected to the heavens, where God was presumed to live. In other words, all of the world above, below, and on the earth is in God, and not even death can separate the dead from the living on the earth and the GOD living in the heavens.

48. Boyer, *Abecedarian of Sacred Trees*, 111.

Psalm Response: "Ascribe to the LORD, O heavenly beings, / ascribe to the LORD glory and strength. / The voice of the LORD flashes forth flames of fire. / The voice of the LORD shakes the wilderness . . . . / The voice of the LORD causes the oaks to whirl, / and strips the forest bare; / and in his temple all say, 'Glory!'" (NRSV, Ps 29:1, 7–8a, 9)

Meditation/Journal: If there is an oak tree—any one of many varieties—near where you live, go to it and sit under it in silence. If there is no oak tree near you, any tall tree will do. Become aware of how its roots reach deep into the earth while its trunk, firmly planted in the earth, elevates its branches and leaves into the heavens. Locate a very small stone and place it under the tree to make you aware of being in the divine presence. Other than in biblical literature, where else in media have you discovered sacred trees that make you aware of being in God (like *The Lord of the Rings, The Chronicles of Narnia,* and *Avatar*)?

Prayer: While gazing on an oak tree, I become aware of your presence, O God, under the earth, on the earth, and in the heavens. Open my ears to hear your voice and loosen my tongue to sing your praise today, tomorrow, and forever. Amen.

Dog

Introduction: Many solitaries keep a dog or a cat or some other pet. Our focus here is on the dog as a sign of the divine presence, while not denying that other domestic pets may serve the same purpose.[49] The dog is a domestic carnivorous animal displaying a long muzzle, pointed ears, a fur coat, a long fur-covered tail, and barks. Usually considered to be a descendent of the wolf, the prophet Isaiah compares Israel's watchmen to them: "They're dogs without sense enough to bark, / lazy dogs, dreaming in the sun—/ But hungry dogs, they do know how to eat, / voracious dogs, with never enough" (Isa 56:10–11a). The author of the book of Proverbs compares a fool to them, writing, "As a dog eats its own vomit, / so fools recycle silliness" (Prov 26:11). And if that were not enough to convince you that the dog was a despised animal in ancient Israel, in the CB (NT) we have the story of the "Greek, Syro-Phoenician" woman, who asks Jesus to heal her daughter, and he replies, "'Stand in line and take your turn. The children get fed first. If there's any left over, the dogs get it. She said, 'Of course, Master. But don't dogs under the table get scraps dropped by the children?'" (Mark 7:26–28). Yes, Jesus refers to this Gentile woman as a dog! However, instead of responding to his negative remark, she stretches his comparison to include Gentiles getting leftover Jewish scraps. And he is impressed with her verbal javelin and rewards her by curing her daughter. The author of Matthew's Gospel records this same story, which he got from his Markan source, and alters it. The Matthean Jesus responds to the Canaanite woman's request, stating, "It's not right to take bread out of children's mouths and throw it to dogs" and she, being quick, states, "You're right, Master, but beggar dogs do get scraps from the master's table" (Matt 15:26–27). As in the Jewish world, so were dogs considered to be unclean in the Muslim world. While dogs are considered to be unclean or negative in most biblical and Muslim literature, this is not the case in the Apocryphal book of Tobit. Before reading the passage from Tobit, watch "God and Dog" by Wendy J. Francisco at https://www.youtube.com/watch?app=desktop&v=H17edn_RZoY—.

Read: Tobit 6:1—12:22

---

49. For more on celebrating animals, especially the dog, see "Dog" in Mark G. Boyer's *An Abecedarian of Animal Spirit Guides: Spiritual Growth through Reflections on Creatures* (Eugene, OR: Wipf and Stock, 2016) 20–28.

Scripture: "At last [Toby and Azariah] were on their way [home]. . . . Azariah had a suggestion . . . 'Let's trot on ahead of the caravan and help prepare [your father's] household for the grand arrival.' Trotting along behind them, as throughout the whole trip, was the faithful family dog" (Tob 11:1, 3, 4c).

Reflection: In the Apocryphal book of Tobit, the family dog is mentioned two times. After Toby finds Azariah, the archangel Raphael in disguise, to accompany him on a trip to retrieve money Toby's father once loaned, to find a cure for Tobit's blindness, and to find a wife for Toby from among his kinsfolk, the novelist writes: "Anna [, Tobit's wife and Toby's mother] stopped crying after her husband's assurances [that Toby would return home] and turned to watch her son as he disappeared on his adventure. Toby and Azariah were in the middle distance now, heading for the horizon. Trailing along after them was the family dog" (Tob 6:1–2a). The dog serves no purpose in the novella other than being a faithful traveling companion. Because the dog is faithful, found in the fact of the dog's return with them in the Scripture passage above, the dog has come to be known as man's best friend and is considered, usually, as a furry member of the modern family.

Roel Sterckx states that in pre-Buddhist China, the dog served as a spiritual medium. "Dogs embodied familiarity and proximity between the human and animal world," he writes.[50] "They lived on the threshold of the realms of the living and the dead, and their mediating role between the domestic world and the world outside is well attested."[51] The dog is a guardian or mediator between the levels of the universe, the underworld and the earth. Similarly, the Egyptian dog-god, Anubis, protected the dead, warding off tomb scavengers, and was credited with the invention of embalming. A statue of Anubis, either in the likeness of a dog or of a man with a dog's head, often was placed in front of tombs.

It is common both in the country and in the city to see people outside walking their dogs. It is also common to see dogs

50. Sterckx, "Tawny Bull," 263.
51. Sterckx, "Tawny Bull," 263.

sitting in cars and trucks and in kennels being taken on flights with their owners. Dogs individually trained to work with or to perform tasks with people with disabilities are known as service dogs, assistance dogs, or therapy dogs. Dogs brought to visit nursing home residents and children in hospitals have a calming effect on those who talk to the dogs and pet them. People adopt dogs from shelters or serve as foster parents for dogs awaiting adoption. In the United States, about 50 percent of households have a dog. Therefore, it comes as no surprise that many solitaries have a dog. Because animals, like people, are in God, they share and manifest the divine. Celebrating a dog (or other pet) can take place on the dog's birthday, adoption day, or any other time that is determined by the solitary. The focus is on the spiritual life that is shared between the solitary and the dog and the manifestation of the divine to the solitary.

Psalm Response: "O LORD, how manifold are your works! / In wisdom you have made them all; / the earth is full of your creatures. / These all look to you / to give them their food in due season; / when you give to them, they gather it up; / when you open your hand, they are filled with good things. / When you hide your face, they are dismayed; / when you take away their breath, they die / and return to their dust. / When you send forth your spirit, they are created; / and you renew the face of the ground" (NRSV, PS 104:24, 27–30).

Meditation/Journal: In your lifetime, what changes have you noted in people's attitudes concerning dogs (or other pets)? If you own a dog, what does the dog reflect to you about the divine presence? If you do not own a dog, what dog do you know—belonging to a friend—that affects your spiritual life? How does the dog do that?

Prayer: As I travel your earth, O LORD, I find myself accompanied by some of the many creatures you have made. Give me a greater respect for all of them, as they manifest something unique about your divine presence. May all of us be your face in this world and in the spirit world, where you live forever and ever. Amen.

Lamp (Light)

Introduction: Before there were candles, there were oil lamps. Clay, ceramic, or metal lamps were usually round, covered, flat vessels, a few inches tall. On one side was a handle, and opposite it was a large spout-like opening into which was placed a reed or cloth or wool wick, which was set on fire. The wick soaked up olive oil, which was poured through a small hole located on the cover of the vessel. Lamps were made in various sizes, that is, in various circumferences depending on their use. In houses before windows were invented, the lamp was the source of light. Some lamps had more than one holder for wicks in order to increase the brightness of the light. While lamps were usually placed on a lampstand, some lamps were made with the lampstand attached. The Markan Jesus asks his listeners: "Does anyone bring a lamp home and put it under a washtub or beneath the bed?" (Mark 4:21a) While his hearers are nodding their heads no, he asks, "Don't you put it up on a table or on the mantel? (Mark 4:21b) And his hearers nod their heads yes. The author of Matthew's Gospel gives the Markan Jesus' words a different setting in the Sermon on the Mount. The Matthean Jesus tells his listeners: "You're here to be light, bringing out the God-colors in the world. . . . If I make you light-bearers, you don't think I'm going to hide you under a bucket, do you? I'm putting you on a light stand. Now that I've put you there on a hilltop, on a light stand—shine!" (Matt 5:14a, 15) The author of Luke's Gospel repeats his Markan source, portraying his Jesus saying: "No one lights a lamp and then covers it with a washtub or shoves it under the bed. No, you set it up on a lamp stand so those who enter the room can see their way" (Luke 8:16) and "No one lights a lamp, then hides it in a drawer. It's put on a lamp stand so those entering the room have light to see where they're going (Luke 11:33).

Unique to Matthew's Gospel is the parable of the five wise and five foolish virgins (Matt 25:1–13). In that account, the author compares the ten young women to the kingdom of God. While all of them took oil lamps with them to go out and greet the bridegroom, five were silly and five were smart. The silly ones carried lamps but no extra oil. The wise women brought jars of oil to feed their lamps. Of course, the bridegroom was delayed for some reason. All ten of the virgins fell asleep. When he finally arrived, the wise ones poured oil into their lamps and got them lit. The foolish ones had no oil to pour into their lamps, and the wise ones didn't have enough for themselves and their foolish counterparts. When the groom arrived, the wise ones with lamps afire went into the wedding feast, while the foolish ones, who had gone to look for oil, were locked out. As in other biblical wedding stories, the bride is conspicuously absent. Thus, this is not an account about a wedding, but it is one about the return of Jesus, the bridegroom, to the earth someday. It says that we need a jar full of oil to be prepared to welcome him.

In a modern version of that parable, Corbin S. Cole and I present four rewritten forms of that parable.[52] We compare the use of ancient lamps to flashlights with batteries, contestants with music for songs, people standing in line to buy tickets for a concert, and miners with batteries for their flashlights. The lesson of each form of the parable is be prepared.

Read: Luke 12:35–40

Scripture: "Keep your shirts on; keep the lights on! Be like house servants waiting for their master to come back from his

---

52. For more on modern parables, especially "Ten Bridesmaids (Virgins)," see Mark G. Boyer's and Corbin S. Cole's *Living Parables: Today's Versions* (Eugene, OR: Wipf and Stock, 2020) 31–34.

honeymoon, awake and ready to open the door when he arrives and knocks" (Luke 12:35–36).

Reflection: A unique Lukan parable exhorts readers to keep the lights on and to stay awake awaiting the return of the master from his honeymoon. Those servants will be blessed, as the usual custom of servants serving their master is reversed, and the master serves them. Keeping a light on means someone is home. "You know that if the house owner had known what night the burglar was coming, he wouldn't have stayed out late and left the place unlocked," states the Lukan Jesus (Luke 12:39). Then, the author of the third gospel makes an application of keeping a light on. He states, "So don't you be slovenly and careless. Just when you don't expect him, the Son of Man will show up" (Luke 12:40). Thus, this is another exhortation about Jesus, the bridegroom's return. Matthew's Gospel contains the same material and makes the same application: ". . . [S]tay awake, alert. You have no idea what day your Master will show up. But you do know this: You know that if the homeowner had known what time of night the burglar would arrive, he would have been there with his dogs to prevent the break-in. Be vigilant just like that. You have no idea when the Son of Man is going to show up" (Matt 23:42–44).

In *Living Parables*, Cole and I present three modern versions of the Lukan parable. We compare keeping the light on and being ready for Jesus' return to children waiting for their parents to come home after a night on the town, to college students waiting for their professor to enter a classroom, and to a man waiting for his wife to return from a business trip. The first part of the Lukan parable about the house owner being awake to keep the burglar from entering his home with its parallel in Matthew's Gospel is compared to a jewelry store owner, the owner of a home to which a parcel delivery truck driver leaves a package (think porch pirates), the owner of a $400,000 home, to people living on an island with active volcanoes, to people upon whom a nuclear weapon is launched, and to a car thief.[53] There is a version of keeping the light

---

53. For more on modern parables, especially "Waiting for the Master" and "Thief" see Mark G. Boyer's and Corbin S. Cole's *Living Parables: Today's Versions* (Eugene, OR: Wipf and Stock, 2020) 65–68.

on and waiting for the burglar in Paul's First Letter to the Thessalonians. The apostle writes: "You know as well as I that the day of the Master's coming can't be posted on our calendars. He won't call ahead and make an appointment any more than a burglar would. About the time everybody's walking around complacently, congratulating each other—'We've sure got it made! Now we can take it easy!'—suddenly everything will fall apart. It's going to come as suddenly and inescapably as birth pangs to a pregnant woman" (1 Thess 5:2–3). Then, Paul reminds his readers: "But friends, you're not in the dark, so how could you be taken off guard by any of this? You're sons of Light, daughters of Day" (1 Thess 5:4–5). There is also a version of keeping the light on and waiting for the burglar in the Gospel of Thomas: "Jesus said: 'Blessed is the person who knows at what point the robbers are entering, so that he may rise up, muster his estate, and arm himself before they enter.'"[54]

The point of the keeping the light on is best summarized by Tom Bodett's Motel 6 advertising slogan: "We'll leave the light on for you." Biblically, in King David's song, are the words, ". . . [Y]ou are my lamp, O LORD, the LORD lightens my darkness" (NRSV, 2 Sam 22:29). Peterson translates that verse: "Suddenly, GOD, your light floods my path, / GOD drives out the darkness" (2 Sam 22:29). "Your word is a lamp to my feet / and a light to my path," sings the psalmist (NRSV, Ps 119:105). Peterson translates that verse: "By your words I can see where I'm going; / they throw a beam of light on my dark path" (Ps 119:105). Turning on a light switch and standing in the beams can make you aware of being in the divine. Lighting a candle in a dark room and watching it flicker presents the opportunity to be aware of being in the divine light. Reading the Bible or another spiritual book or article that gives you insight, that raises your awareness to being in God, gives you words that light your dark way. Be light! Shine! Glow with the divinity you share! Be aware and let no burglar extinguish your light!

Psalm Response: "I love you, O LORD, my strength. / I call upon the LORD, who is worthy to be praised . . . . It is you who light my

54. Ehrman and Plese, *Apocryphal Gospels*, 333.

lamp; / the LORD, my God, lights up my darkness" (NRSV, Ps 18:1, 3, 28).

Meditation/Journal: Go through your home and count the number of table lamps, floor lamps, and night lights you have. How does each table lamp, floor lamp, and night light make you aware that you are in God? In what specific ways are you a light-bearer, shining the divine presence on your pet and others who may visit you?

Prayer: I share your divine light, O God, and your lamp burns with the oil of my life. Grant me greater awareness of your presence every time I turn on a lamp or light a candle to scatter the darkness today, tomorrow, and forever. Amen.

Clothing

Introduction: While the concept is no longer true, people seventy years ago used to separate their clothing into weekday and Sunday wear. Weekday clothes were worn to work and around the house Monday through Saturday. Sunday clothes were reserved for wear to church, weddings, and funerals. Clothes are garments that cover the body; they vary in style from one generation to the next and from one epoch to another. The sheets, quilts, and blankets that cover a bed are often called bed clothes. The word *clothes* comes from the word *cloth*, the fabric out of which clothes are made. Before putting on clean clothes, people usually take a bath or shower; in other words, they wash their body clean before decorating it with clean clothes.

The Bible attributes clothing to God: "GOD made leather clothing for Adam and his wife and dressed them," states the HB (OT) book of Genesis (3:21). God makes clothing because, after hearing "the sound of GOD strolling in the garden in the evening breeze" (Gen 3:8), Adam and Eve hide in the trees of the garden. Adam says, "I heard you in the garden and I was afraid because I was naked. And I hid" (Gen 3:10). The narrative in Genesis is less about the origin of wearing clothing and more about the practice of doing so at the time the biblical book was written. John McKenzie states, "The Hebrews regarded nudity as extremely shameful. . . ."[55] God tells Isaiah son of Amoz, "'Go, take off your clothes and sandals,' and Isaiah did it, going about naked and barefooted" (Isa 20:2). Then God explained that Isaiah was a sign that the Assyrians were going to invade Israel and "take young and old alike and march them out of there naked and barefooted . . ." (Isa 20:4). Similarly, the prophet Amos refers to captives of war being marched naked; the bravest of warriors, writes Amos, won't make it. "He'll run off for dear life, stripped naked . . ." (Amos 2:15). Nakedness represented shame. The Romans conducted capital executions—crucifixions—and stripped off all the prisoner's clothes. Thus, depending on the climate, men wore wrap-around kilts and both men and women wore bath-robe like, ankle-length gowns made of wool or linen. Both sexes may have also worn a head covering with or without a veil attached. Over those clothes, one could wear a cloak or mantle to keep warm. Both sexes may possess a festive garment that was worn for a special occasion.

In HB (OT) history, the concept of clean and unclean is associated with clean clothes. Being clean did not mean not being dirty; it meant being free from any physical, moral, or ritual contamination. Uncleanness came about through eating food from unclean animals (such as the camel or pig), through skin diseases (such as leprosy, psoriasis, rash), contact with a dead body, and bodily fluids (such as blood or semen). Most uncleanness could be removed by taking a bath or the passage of time. This understanding explains why GOD says to Moses on Mount Sinai

55. McKenzie, *Dictionary*, 143.

(Horeb), "For the next two days get these people ready to meet the Holy GOD. Have them scrub their clothes so that on the third day they'll be fully prepared, because on the third day GOD will come down on Mount Sinai and make his presence known to all the people" (Exod 19:10b–11). The narrator of the HB (OT) book of Exodus, states: "Moses went down the mountain to the people and prepared them for the holy meeting. They gave their clothes a good scrubbing" (Exod 19:14). If the Hebrews (Israelites) had incurred any uncleanness, by washing their clothes they would become clean and ready to experience the presence of God.

Another biblical action is tearing one's clothes. Tearing clothes is a physical and visible expression of grief in the face of death and/or anger. Changing clothes indicates a change in the way of living; for example, after being cured, a person was readmitted to society and changed his or her clothes. In the account about Joseph, son of Jacob, and his ability to interpret Pharaoh's dreams, after being summoned by Pharoah, Joseph is released from prison and puts on clean clothes before appearing before the ruler of Egypt.

Read: Genesis 41:1–46

Scripture: "Pharaoh at once sent for Joseph. They brought him on the run from the jail cell. He cut his hair, put on clean clothes, and came to Pharaoh" (Gen 41:14).

Reflection: The novella concerning Jacob's sons selling their brother into slavery in Egypt occupies the last chapters (37–50) of the book of Genesis. Joseph's brothers are jealous of him and his cloak of many colors given to him by their father, Jacob. So, they hatch a plot to sell him to salvers going to Egypt. Once Joseph gets to Egypt, he is bought by Potiphar, an Egyptian official, as a slave. Potiphar puts him in charge of his household, but Potiphar's wife attempts to seduce him. When he refuses to sleep with her, she accuses him of the very crime she attempted to get him to commit. As a result, Joseph is imprisoned. While there, he accurately interprets dreams that the Pharaoh's cupbearer and baker have. Two years later, the cupbearer remembers him to Pharoah, after the king has dreams which none of his officials could interpret.

Once Joseph puts on clean clothes and appears before Pharoah, he accurately interprets the king of Egypt's dreams, but attributes his ability to do so to God. Nevertheless, Pharoah puts Joseph in charge of the entire country in order to prepare for an imminent famine. Then, Pharoah puts his signet ring on Joseph's finger to indicate that he is now second in command to Pharoah. "He outfitted him in robes of the best linen . . ." (Gen 41:42). Joseph has gone from shepherd to slave to prisoner to assistant Pharoah, and a change of clothes signifies his new way of life.

In most cultures, such as illustrated in the biblical culture, nakedness in public is not acceptable, except in places where it is legally permitted, such as clothing-optional or nude beaches or nudist camps or colonies. Propriety, based on custom and law, dictates where nudity is acceptable or not acceptable. Near nudity can be observed in the skimpy swim suits that many people wear on a beach. That should come as no surprise, as ancient fishermen usually worked in the nude. However, even nudists put on clothes when leaving their residences and entering general society. Among the general public, shame is still associated with nudity either directly or indirectly. While nudity may be the occasion for awareness of being in God and created in the image of the divine, the focus of this reflection is on washing clothes and putting on clean or festive clothes as an occasion to be aware of the divine presence. Some people have a predetermined day of the week when they do laundry; some wash clothes only when they need to do so. Washing clothes and putting on clean clothes can awaken us to being in God, to being in the divine presence.

Psalm Response: "O my God, . . . [Y]ou are holy, / enthroned on the praises of Israel. / In you our ancestors trusted; / they trusted, and you delivered them. / To you they cried, and were saved; / in you they trusted, and were not put to shame. / . . . [I]t was you who took me from the womb; / and kept me safe on my mother's breast. / On you I was cast from my birth, / and since my mother bore me you have been my God. / Do not be far from me, for trouble is near / and there is no one to help. / [My enemies] divide my clothes among themselves/ and for my clothing they cast lots. / But you, O

LORD, do not be far away! / O my help, come quickly to my aid!" (NRSV, Ps 22:2a, 3–5, 9–11, 18–19)

Meditation/Journal: When do you wash your clothes (do laundry)? What part of washing clothes has the potential to enhance your spirituality by making you aware of being in God? When do you purchase new clothes? What do they signify to you? What aspect of owning new clothes can enhance your spirituality by raising your awareness of being in God?

Prayer: After you created people in your own image, O God, you sewed clothes for them to cover their shame and to reveal your encompassing presence to them. Pour your grace upon me and make me aware that the clothes I wash and wear bring me into your presence now and forever. Amen.

Ring

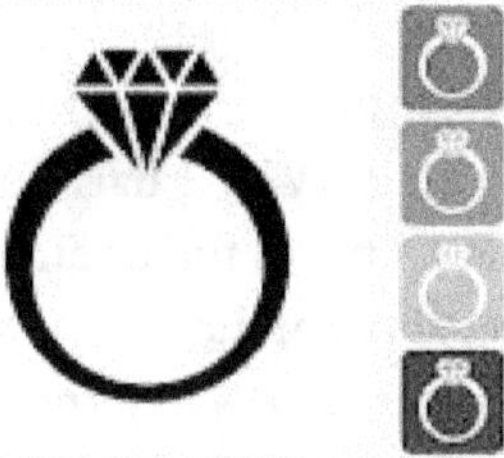

Introduction: In our world, people wear a variety of rings. The usual ones are those on fingers and ears—top, center, and bottom. However, it is not uncommon to see people with rings in or through their nose, on their toes, through an eyebrow, tongue, or lips, hanging from nipples, penises, and scrotums, and elsewhere. Usually, one person proposing marriage to another presents a ring for the other's ring finger (left hand, third finger from the thumb). Unless the engagement is broken at a later date for some reason, the ring signifies the commitment of one person to marry another. In other words, the ring represents commitment; it is a pledge.

In the biblical world, there are three kinds of rings worn by people. Earrings, fashioned from gold, silver, or something else, are worn by both men and women. The author of the book of Genesis recounts Jacob collecting from his family "their lucky-charm earrings" (Gen 35:4). Likewise, the author of the book of Exodus portrays Aaron, brother of Moses, collecting "the gold rings from the ears of [the] wives and sons and daughters" of those men who left Egypt in order to make a calf of gold (Exod 32:2–3). Later, Moses collected earrings—among other things made of gold—from both men and women to make the tabernacle and its furnishings (Gen 35:1–29). The prophet Ezekiel mentions "sapphire earrings," among other things, that God gave to his people (Ezek 16:12). As can be concluded from those texts, both females and males wore earrings.

Second, a ring worn on a person's finger was usually a signet ring found on the hand of kings and other officials. The signet ring was a small seal engraved on a ring used to make an impression in wax on a document. According to the *Dictionary of Biblical Imagery*, ". . . [T]he ownership of [a signet] ring was synonymous with power."[56] This is illustrated in the account of Pharaoh placing Joseph in charge of Egypt to prepare for the imminent famine that was coming to the country. The narrator states, ". . . Pharaoh removed his signet ring from his finger and slipped it on Joseph's hand. . . . Joseph was in charge of the entire country of Egypt" (Gen 41:42–43b). Likewise, in the short story known as Esther, once Haman's plot to eliminate the Jews is revealed to King Ahasuerus by Queen Esther, the narrator states, ". . . [T]he king took off his signet ring, which he had taken from Haman, and gave it to Mordecai," Esther's cousin and adoptive father (Esth 8:2). Then, in order to undo the plot to kill Jews, the king instructs Queen Esther, a Jewess, and Mordecai to write letters cancelling Haman's instructions in his name as king "and seal the letters with [his] ring, which will guarantee the contents of the edict" (Esth 8:8). The prophet Isaiah mentions signet rings among the things that God will take away from his people (Isa 3:21), although Peterson refers to them as "the rings on their fingers" (Isa 3:21). The prophet Ezekiel mentions

56. Ryken, Wilhoit, and Longman, *Dictionary*, 728.

"emerald rings" (Ezek16:12) being among the gifts God gave to his people. The unique parable in Luke's Gospel about the lost son portrays the boy's father restoring him to his place in the family by putting the family ring on his finger (Luke 15:22), when the son returns home after squandering his inheritance.

The third kind of ring was a nose ring, which will be discussed in the reflection below.

Read: Genesis 24:1–67

Scripture: Abraham's senior servant "brought out gifts, [among them was] a gold nose ring weighing a little over a quarter of an ounce and . . . gave [it] to [Rebekah]" (Gen 24:22). Later in the story as the servant recounts the successive events leading to his meeting with Rebekah to Laban, Rebekah's brother, he says, "I gave her a ring for her nose . . . ." (Gen 24:47b)

Reflection: Abraham's senior servant is sent to Abraham's relatives to find a wife for his son, Isaac. The servant, after a series of prayers, finds Rebekah, Abraham's niece, and gives her several valuable gifts, which proves his master's wealth, and a nose ring, a sign that a marriage proposal is being negotiated between the servant (representing Abraham) and Laban (representing his father, Bethuel). A nose ring is a ring that is put through an animal's nose, most often bulls and cows. They are used to wean young cattle by preventing suckling, and they are used on pigs to discourage rooting. They are usually installed through a pierced hole in the nasal septum or rim of the nose. In a patriarchal society, the significance of the nose ring ornament given to a young woman is not to be lost. Leland Ryken, James Wilhoit, and Tremper Longman state, ". . . [B]iblical imagery of a hook in the nose symbolizes mastery or forced leading."[57] In other words, Abraham's servant claims Rebekah for Isaac; it is similar to one person presenting a ring to another upon engagement. Rebekah's acceptance of the nose ring indicates her acceptance of the marriage proposal, as it is narrated in the story.

---

57. Ryken, Wilhoit, and Longman, *Dictionary*, 597.

The fact that the nose ring is inserted in the nose reminds the reader that life is associated with the nose. "GOD formed Man out of dirt from the ground and blew into his nostrils the breath of life. The Man came alive—a living soul!" records the author of Genesis (2:7). Job expresses the same idea, saying: ". . . [F]or as long as I draw breath, / and for as long as God breathes life into me, / I refuse to say one word that isn't true" (Job 27:3). Ryken, Wilhoit, and Longman state, "Every living thing has the breath of life in its nostrils, but only man [and woman] has the breath of God in his [or her] nostrils."[58] Thus, the ring signifies the commitment of Rebekah to Isaac and the new life that they will bring forth through their imminent marriage.

Today, a nose ring is not a sign of engagement or commitment, unless it is made so by the two people getting engaged. Today, a nose ring is an ornament worn usually to decorate the female body. A ring presented to and placed on the left-hand ring finger in an engagement ceremony (usually consisting of a meal with wine or champagne eaten in a restaurant or during or after dancing) signifies two peoples' commitment to each other. A ring may be worn by a solitary, usually on the right-hand ring finger, but not exclusively, to represent his or her commitment to developing a solitary spirituality way of life. The commitment may be for a short time, a long time, or a lifetime. The length is determined by the solitary. Before beginning a solitary existence or while living a solitary life, a person may choose to celebrate his or her commitment to using the ring as an awareness of being in God. All that is needed is the ring already placed on a finger or prepared to be placed on a finger.

Psalm Response: "You who live in the shelter of the Most High, / who abide in the shadow of the Almighty, / will say to the LORD, 'My refuge and my fortress; / my God, in whom I trust.' / Because you have made the LORD you refuge, / the Most High your dwelling place, / no evil shall befall you, / . . . Those who love me [, the LORD], I will deliver; / I will protect those who know my name. /

---

58. Ryken, Wilhoit, and Longman, *Dictionary*, 597.

When they call to me, I will answer them; / I will be with them in trouble, / I will rescue them and honor them. / With long life I will satisfy them, / and show them my salvation" (NRSV, Ps 91:1–2, 9–10a, 14–16).

Meditation/Journal: When did you first commit yourself to solitary spirituality? Did you place a ring on your finger to commemorate the commitment? Specifically, what does the ring represent for you?

Prayer: LORD God, you breathe your life into me so that I may be filled with your Spirit. Grant me a long life full of spiritual insight and grace, and grant that one day I will see your face, for I live and move and having my being in you now and forever. Amen.

Fire

Introduction: At various times and in various cultures around the world, fire is celebrated. It is not uncommon to see bonfires lit the evening before Halloween or on Halloween itself. Many people have a chiminea in their back yard in which is burned wood for warmth on a chilly evening. Likewise, across the land we see portable fire pits or metal baskets in which fires are kindled and around which people gather for warmth outside on a cold evening. God manifests himself as fire to Moses, who was shepherding his father-in-law's flock near Mount Horeb (Sinai). "The angel of GOD appeared to him in flames of fire blazing out of the middle of a bush. He looked. The bush was blazing away but it didn't burn up" (Exod 3:2). The narrator of the event in the HB (OT) book of Exodus continues: "Moses said, 'What's going on here? I can't believe this! Amazing! Why doesn't the bush burn up?' GOD saw that he had stopped to look. God called to him from out of the bush, 'Moses! Moses!' He said, 'Yes? I'm right here!'" (Exod 3:3–4)

Moses' life changes dramatically after encountering God as fire. He is changed from a sheep and goat herder to a leader of his Hebrew people, who are Egyptian slaves. After battles with Pharaoh, he leads the slaves out of Egypt to freedom. And along the way to the land promised to Abraham and his descendants by God, according to the biblical author, "GOD went ahead of them in a Pillar of Cloud during the day to guide them on the way, and at night in a Pillar of Fire to give them light; thus they could travel both day and night. The Pillar of Cloud by day and the Pillar of fire by night never left the people" (Exod 13:21–22).

In a similar way, God manifested his presence to Gideon in the book of Judges. The angel of GOD—a biblical code for God—appears to Gideon, while he is threshing wheat and calls him to lead his people in battle against his enemies, the Midianites. After God promises to be with him, Gideon says to God, "If you're serious about this, do me a favor: Give me a sign to back up what you're telling me. Don't leave until I come back and bring you my gift" (Judg 6:17–18a). Gideon goes and prepares a sacrifice of goat, bread, and broth. He brings them to God in the form of the angel. The angel directs him how to prepare the sacred meal on a rock. "The angel of GOD stretched out the tip of the stick he was holding and touched the meat and the bread. Fire broke out of the rock and burned up the meat and bread while the angel of God slipped out of sight. And Gideon knew it was the angel of God!" (Judg 6:21–22)

The prophet Isaiah also experiences God as fire. ". . . I've looked God in the face!" states the prophet (Isa 6:5). Then, he narrates: ". . . [O]ne of the angel-seraphs flew to me. He held a live coal that he had taken with tongs from the altar. He touched my mouth with the coal and said, 'Look. This coal has touched your lips. . . . And then I heard the voice of the Master: 'Whom shall I send? Who will go for us?' I spoke up, "I'll go. Send me!'" (Isa 6:6–7a, 8)

Because of all the biblical stories portraying God as fire, a celebration of fire is a celebration of the God in whom we live and move and have our being.[59] All that is needed for a fire in a wood fireplace is paper, kindling, wood, and matches. If the fireplace has gas logs, then one only has to turn them on. Outside, a fire can be built in an earthen pit surrounded with stones or concrete blocks or pavers with paper, kindling, wood, and matches; a small fire can also be built in a chiminea or metal fire pit or basket. Once the fire is started, stand or sit near it and watch the flames lick the wood and consume it or watch the flames dance on the gas logs.

Read: 1 Kings 18:1–39

Scripture: "When it was time for the sacrifice to be offered, Elijah the prophet came up [Mount Carmel] and prayed, 'O GOD, God of Abraham, Isaac, and Israel, make it known right now that you are God in Israel, that I am your servant, and that I'm doing what I'm doing under your orders. Answer me, GOD; O answer me and reveal to this people that you are GOD, the true God, and that you are giving these people another chance at repentance.' Immediately the fire of GOD fell and burned up the offering, the wood, the stones, the dirt, and even the water in the trench. All the people saw it happen and fell on their faces in awed worship, exclaiming, 'GOD is the true God. GOD is the true God!'" (1 Kgs 18:36–39)

Reflection: Chapter 18 of the First Book of Kings presents dueling prophets: eight hundred fifty prophets of Baal and Asherah versus the one prophet of God: Elijah. The purpose of the duel is to bring an end to a severe drought. The reader has to know that Baal is a fertility god, who is responsible for the agricultural fertility of the area, which includes rain. In order to prove to the people who the real God is, Elijah suggests a contest.

The prophets of each god would get an ox to be sacrificed on an altar on firewood. No fire would be ignited. Rather, each would pray to his god, and whichever god answered the prayer with fire

---

59. For many celebrations of fire, see Mark G. Boyer's *Nature Spirituality: Praying with Wind, Water, Earth, Fire* (Eugene, OR: Resource, Publications, 2013) especially pages 101–35.

would prove to be the true fertility god. The eight hundred fifty prophets are first to prepare their offering. Then, they prayed all morning, but nothing happened. Elijah taunted them by suggesting that their god may be off meditating, working on a project, on vacation, or overslept.

Then, Elijah took command of the situation. He built an altar out of twelve stones, laid firewood on the altar, and put the cut-up ox on the wood. He also dug a trench all around the altar. Then, for three times he had four buckets of water poured over the ox and firewood until the trench was full of water. Elijah prays, and God acts: Fire burns the wet offering; even the stones, dirt, and water in the trench disappear! There is no doubt who the real God is; he has manifested his presence as fire—again.

The narrator of this account has been telling the reader who the real God is throughout the telling of the story. Elijah uses twelve stones to build his altar. Those twelve stone represent the twelve tribes of Israel (Jacob's sons); Jacob, son of Isaac, son of Abraham, served the real God and inherited the promises that God made concerning life, freedom, and the very land upon which they were standing! To further emphasize his point, the narrator states that three times four buckets of water were poured over the ox, wood, and stones, until the trench around it all was filled with water. Four times three are twelve. Twelve in the HB (OT) represent the people God chose as his own and with Moses as their guide led them out of Egyptian slavery to the freedom of the land promised to Abraham, Isaac, and Jacob. Twelve in the CB (NT) represents the new people God has chosen through Jesus, God made flesh. Thus, the number twelve is not about twelve of anything (since there were never twelve tribes nor were there only twelve apostles); it is a number signifying people God has chosen to be his own.

Furthermore, the slaughtered oxen blood echo the bull's blood used by Moses to ratify the covenant between God and the people at the foot of Mount Horeb (Sinai). Some of the blood was splashed on the altar, and some was sprinkled on the people. God and people became blood brothers and sisters. In the CB (NT) Emmanuel, God-with-us, Jesus takes a cup of wine during the Passover meal and says to those gathered around him, "This is my blood, / God's . . . covenant, / Poured out for many people" (Mark 14:24; see Matt 26:28; Luke 22:20). Blood, representing divine life, is sprinkled or consumed by people. In other words, the very divinity in whom they live and move and have their being is within them.

To further enhance the divine presence, the narrator of the story tells the reader that it was at the time for the evening sacrifice that God accepts Elijah's offering through fire. In the evening both at the shrine of the ark of the covenant and, later, in the Temple, a burned-up sacrifice was made to God. On Mount Carmel, the all-encompassing presence of God is nearer than the people could have imagined. They shout, "GOD is the true God!" and they bow down and worship the God who is there with them in whose presence no other god's prophets have a chance.[60]

After Elijah orders the eight-hundred fifty prophets destroyed, it begins to rain, proving that GOD is the true God (1 Kings 18:41, 44–46). Elijah's God is the real fertility God, not Baal or Asherah. Elijah's God gives life, and all that life exists in him. Even the falling rain seems to shout, "GOD is the true God!"

Later in the Elijah cycle of stories, "a chariot and horses of fire came . . . and Elijah went up in a whirlwind to heaven" (2 Kgs 2:11). The God who manifested himself as fire appeared as a chariot and horses of fire and incorporated Elijah into himself using fire. The prophet who had been so aware that he existed in the divine was divinized; all that was left of Elijah was his cloak, which his successor, Elisha, retrieved.

Psalm Response: "Bless the LORD, O my soul. / O LORD my God, you are very great. / You are clothed with honor and majesty, / wrapped in light as with a garment. / You stretch out the heavens like a tent, / you set the beams of your chambers on the waters, / you make the clouds your chariot, / you ride on the wings of the wind, / you make the winds your messengers, / fire and flame your ministers" (NRSV, Ps 104:1–4).

60. For more on divine manifestations, see Mark G. Boyer's *Divine Presence: Elements of Biblical Theophanies* (Eugene, OR: Wipf and Stock, 2017).

Meditation/Journal: What does fire signify to you? Where have you seen God manifested as fire? How did your life change as a result of that vision? How does fire protect you? comfort you?

Prayer: You make your presence known, O God, in fire. Make me deeply aware of how all you have created exists in your fiery voice which flashes forth as lightning, fire in the sky. Like your Son's followers of old, pour on me the flames of your Spirit, and when my time here is done, gather me to you in a chariot with fiery horses. All glory be yours now and forever. Amen.

Wind

Introduction: Many people pay no attention to the wind. Yet, there are days when there is no wind, and there are days when the wind blows furiously. There are even days when a gentle breeze stirs the leaves of the trees or sends snow to carpet the grass. In Hebrew, the original language of much of the HB (OT), the word for wind, breath, air, and spirit is *ruah*—the same word! In Greek, the original language of the CB (NT), the word for wind, breath, air, and spirit is *pneuma*—again, the same word. How those words are translated into English depends on the context of the word as determined by the translator.[61]

We find this in the unique dialogue between Jesus and Nicodemus in John's Gospel. During their discussion about being born again, Jesus says to Nicodemus: "You know well enough how

61. For more on this topic, see Mark G. Boyer's *What is Born of the Spirit is Spirit: A Biblical Spirituality of Spirit* (Eugene, OR: Wipf and Stock, 2019).

the wind blows this way and that. You hear it rustling through the trees, but you have no idea where it comes from or where it's headed next. That's the way it is with everyone 'born from above' by the wind of God, the Spirit of God" (John 3:8). Jesus' words echo those of the narrator of the HB (OT) book of Genesis: "God's Spirit brooded like a bird above the watery abyss" (Gen 1:2). The NRSV translates that verse as "a wind from God swept over the face of the waters" with a footnote stating that it can also be translated as "the spirit of God" or "a mighty wind" swept over the waters. The variety of translations depends on what the translator thinks the writer originally intended to say. Nevertheless, the Johannine Jesus makes clear, "The Spirit can make life" (John 6:63a). That is similar to the narrator's statement in the book of Genesis: ". . . GOD formed Man out of dirt from the ground and blew into his nostrils the breath of life. The Man came alive—a living soul" (Gen 2:7).

We find the same comparison of Spirit to wind in the narrative that has come to be called Pentecost in the CB (NT) Acts of the Apostles. The author—the same as that of the Gospel according to Luke—writes: "Without warning there was a sound like a strong wind, gale force—no one could tell where it came from. It filled the whole building. Then, like a wildfire, the Holy Spirit spread through [the followers of Jesus'] ranks . . ." (Acts 2:2–4). In contrast, the prophet Elijah doesn't experience the divine as "a hurricane wind," but as "a gentle and quiet whisper" (1 Kgs 19:11b, 12). In other words, people become aware that they are in God, who is Spirit, by the wind—no matter if it is strong gale or a gentle breeze.

Read: Ezekiel 37:1–14

Scripture: "[GOD] said to me [, Ezekiel], 'Prophesy to the breath. Prophesy, son of man. Tell the breath, "GOD, the Master, says, Come from the four winds. Come, breath. Breathe on these slain bodies. Breathe life!"'" (Ezek 37:9)

Reflection: The prophet Ezekiel is famous for his enacted prophesies. An enacted prophesy is a primitive type of visual aid during which a dramatic action accompanies the prophet's words. Such is the case of the unique account of Ezekiel's vision of a plain of bones that come alive. As the author makes clear, God grabbed him, but it is God's Spirit that takes him and sets him in the middle of an open plain strewn with bones (Ezek 37:1). Ezekiel walks among the dry bones—bleached by the sun—as if walking through an old battlefield where none of the bodies have ever been buried (Ezek 37:2). The historical Ezekiel went into exile in Babylon with his fellow Israelites after King Nebuchadnezzar captured and destroyed Jerusalem and its Temple in 587 BCE. The bones on the plain represent not only the death of the soldiers who fought Nebuchadnezzar's army, but those Jews taken as captives of war to Babylon. Ezekiel's vision gives hope to the captives that one day they will be set free to return to Jerusalem. As the prophet narrates, "The breath entered them and they came alive! They stood up on their feet, a huge army" (Ezek 37:10). Then, just to make sure that Ezekiel understands, God tells him that the bones represent the house of Israel. God promises that he will open their graves and bring them out alive. They will, and they did, return to their land, because God breathed life into them. In Ezekiel's vision, the captives are immersed in breath, wind, and Spirit—God—in whom they live and move and have their existence.

Psalm 104, a song of praise for God's works, sings about every animal's dependence upon God for life, equating breath and spirit. "Take back your Spirit and they die, / revert to original mud; / Send out your Spirit and they spring to life . . . ," sings the psalmist (Ps 104:29–30). Basically, what the song-writer says is that everyone and everything is in God, who creates all and fills all with breath, God's own Spirit.

More than any other biblical writer, Ezekiel records his experiences of being in God's Spirit. When God speaks to him, spirit enters into him (Ezek 2:2; 3:24), lifts him up (Ezek 3:12, 14; 8:3; 11:1, 24; 43:5), falls upon him (Ezek 11:15), or is put within him (Ezek 37:14). In the CB (NT) Paul states, ". . . [T]he Spirit searches everything, even the depths of God. . . . [N]o one comprehends what is truly God's except the Spirit of God" (NRSV, 1 Cor 2:10, 11b). The goal of spirituality is the awareness, brought to us by the wind, that we live in the Spirit, in God, who gives us life, even if we appear to be or are dead.

Psalm Response: O LORD, "Where can I go from your spirit? / Or where can I flee from your presence? / If I ascend to heaven, you are there . . . . / If I take the wings of the morning / and settle at the farthest limits of the sea, / even there your hand shall lead me, / and your right hand shall hold me fast. / If I say, 'Surely the darkness shall cover me, / and the light around me become night,' / even the darkness is not dark to you; / the night is as bright as the day, / for darkness is as light to you" (NRSV, Ps 139: 7–8a, 9–12).

Meditation/Journal: When has the wind made you aware of being in God's Spirit. When has the wind breathed life into you? When has the wind breathed Spirit into you? How can windchimes remind you of being in God?

Prayer: Just as the wind roams over the earth stirring breath, your Spirit inhabits all living things, O God. Grant me a deeper awareness of how all life-breath comes from you, when I hear the wind blow, and from the four winds send your Spirit to enliven me today, tomorrow, and forever. Amen.

Music

Introduction: A celebration of music of any kind—sacred, classical, modern—is appropriate for the solitary. Music makes us aware that we are in the divine; it alerts us that we live in the divine, just like the music and dancing alerted the elder son in Luke's

Gospel (15:25) that a celebration was taking place. The author of the First Book of Samuel narrates, ". . . [A]fter David had killed the Philistine [Goliath], the women poured out of all the villages of Israel singing and dancing, welcoming King Saul with tambourines, festive songs, and lutes" (1 Sam 18:6). The women celebrated the defeat of Israel's enemy by making music; the men were in the army and joined in the festivities with their king and their wives and daughters.

The A (OT) book of Sirach advises, "Music has no place during the mourning period" (Sir 22:6). Indeed, after King Nebuchadnezzar destroyed Jerusalem, the author of the HB (OT) book of Lamentations declares, "Music from the young is heard no more" (Lam 5:14b). According to Sirach, in its author's praise of "the giants who've gone before us" (Sir 44:1), "the early governors and judges, men and women of great authority, empowered by their own prudence, encouraging the prophets, . . . ruled the people with good counsel, knowledge gained from Scripture, words of wisdom from everyday life—accompanied by lots of singing and psalms and Scripture stories." (Sir 44:3–5).

Music plays a key role in King Nebuchadnezzar's dedication ceremony of a gold statue narrated in the book of Daniel. After all the people have arrived for the ceremony, "A herald . . . proclaimed in a loud voice: 'Attention, everyone! Every race, color, and creed, listen! When you hear the band strike-up—all the trumpets and trombones, the tubas and baritones, the drums and cymbals—fall to your knees and worship the gold statue that King Nebuchadnezzar has set up. Anyone who does not kneel and worship shall be thrown immediately into a roaring furnace'" (Dan 3:4–6). Of course, the Jewish lads—Shadrach (Hananiah), Meshach (Mishael) and Abednego (Azariah)—would not bow in worship to the false god. Tattle-tales in the crowd report to the king that the three Jews he has placed in high positions in Babylon did not follow the command (Dan 3:8–12). The king asks to see them, and they are brought into this presence. He questions them about their refusal to worship the gold statue, even giving them a second chance to do so in order to escape being tossed into the fiery furnace. The three young men answer the king in chorus, declaring that his threat means nothing to them. Thus, Nebuchadnezzar orders the furnace "fired up seven times hotter than usual" (Dan 3:19b). The astute reader will immediately note that the use of fire and the number seven indicates God's presence. The three (indicating God)[62] young men are about to be tossed into God! Of course, nothing will hurt or destroy them. "The three young men danced in the middle of the flames, praising God and blessing the Lord. One of them Azariah, also called Abednego, stopped for a moment and, as the flames were licking his lips, raised his voice in prayer. 'Blessed are you, O Lord, God of our ancestors! You alone are praiseworthy, and your name will be blessed forever!'" (Dan 3:24–26) Once Azariah's twenty-verse hymn of praise is finished, the narrator states, ". . . [I]nside the fire, an angel of the Lord descended upon Azariah and his friends and snuffed the fiery flames, leaving behind a light summer breeze. Apparently, the fire hadn't touched the young men at all or caused them any pain" (Dan 3:49–50a; [Sg Three 26–27a]). This leads the three young men into a long praise of God (Dan 3:52–90; [Sg Three 28–68]). Thus, even though "[t]he band started to play, a huge band equipped with all musical instruments of Babylon, and everyone—every race, color, and creed—fell to their knees and worshiped the gold statue that King Nebuchadnezzar has set up" (Dan 3:7), the three young men did not succumb to the music because they had been placed securely in their God, who saved their lives.

Read: 1 Chr 15:1—16:36

Scripture: ". . . [A]ll Israel brought up the ark of the covenant of the LORD with shouting, to the sound of the horn, trumpets, and cymbals, and made loud music on harps and lyres" (1 Chr 15:28).

Reflection: Other than the book of Psalms, the First Book of Chronicles may contain the most music in the HB (OT). It begins in chapter 6 by mentioning "the persons David appointed to lead the singing in the house of GOD after the Chest [Ark] was placed there" (1 Chr 6:31). After David finished building himself a palace

---

62. Boyer, *Divine Presence*, 10–12.

in Jerusalem, he decided to bring the Ark of the Covenant—the chest containing the tablets of the Law, maybe Moses staff, and maybe a jar of manna—from the home of Obed-Edom, where it was enshrined, to Jerusalem, the capital of the united confederacy of tribes. David prepared a tent. According to First Chronicles, "David then called everyone in Israel to assemble in Jerusalem to bring up the Chest of GOD to its specially prepared place" (1 Chr 15:9). "David ordered the heads of the Levites to assign their relatives to sing in the choir, accompanied by a well-equipped marching band, and fill the air with joyful sound" (1 Chr 15:16). First Chronicles draws a picture of the procession: "On they came, all Israel on parade bringing up the Chest of the Covenant of GOD, shouting and cheering, playing every kind of brass and percussion and string instrument" (1 Chr 15:28). The narrator continues: "They brought the Chest of God and placed it right in the center of the tent that David had pitched for it; then they worshiped . . ." (1 Chr 16:1). Thus, David seals his power as king in his new capital city (Jerusalem) with God living in it.

Once the Chest (Ark) is in place in Jerusalem, King David has not only solidified his position as monarch, but he now has God on his side, living in his capital city. The next item on David's to-do list is to assemble worship leaders and select some for special service in preaching and teaching music (1 Chr 25:1). NRSV states that they would "prophesy with lyres, harps, and cymbals" (NRSV, 1 Chr 25:1). First Chronicles mentions one family of six sons, who "were supervised by their father Jeduthn, who preached and accompanied himself with the zither—he was responsible for leading the thanks and praise or GOD." (1 Chr 25:3). Another family of fourteen sons and three daughters are under their father Heman's supervision, and "they were in charge of leading the singing and providing musical accompaniment in the work of worship in the sanctuary of God" (1 Chr 25:6).

After David's son, Solomon, builds the Temple in Jerusalem, the Second Book of Chronicles narrates the procession of the Chest (Ark) from the tent, where David had enthroned it, to the Temple's Inner Sanctuary, the Holy of Holies. At this point in time, the chronicler states, "There was nothing in the Chest itself but the two stone tablets that Moses had placed in it at Horeb where GOD made a covenant with Israel after bringing them up from Egypt" (2 Chr 5:10). Then, Second Chronicles notes that all the Levites who were musicians, the choir, and the orchestra assembled on the east side of the Altar and were joined by 120 priests blowing trumpets (2 Chr 5:12). "The choir and trumpets made one voice of praise and thanks to GOD—orchestra and choir in perfect harmony singing and playing praise to GOD: Yes! God is good! His loyal love goes on forever! Then a billowing cloud filled The Temple of GOD. The priests couldn't even carry out their duties because of the cloud—the glory of GOD!—that filled The Temple of God" (2 Chr 5:13–14).

Psalm 68 captures some of the excitement of the procession. "See God on parade / to the sanctuary, my God, / my King on the march!" sings the psalmist. Then, the psalmist gives the order of the procession: "Singers out front, the band behind, / maidens in the middle with castanets. / The whole choir blesses God. / Like a fountain of praise, Israel blesses GOD" (Ps 68:24–26). The author of Psalm 92 focuses more on the musical instruments being played. "What a beautiful thing, GOD, to give thanks, / to sing an anthem to you, the High God! / To announce your love each daybreak, / sing your faithful presence all through the night, / Accompanied by dulcimer and harp, / the full-bodied music of strings" (Ps 92:1–3).

Just as music surrounds those who are near its source, so are they in God. Think of the vibration that comes from loud music, especially drums and electric guitars. Singing, playing a musical instrument, or listening to music can awaken us to being in God.

Psalm Response: "Hear this, all you peoples; / give ear, all inhabitants of the world, both low and high, / rich and poor together. / My mouth shall speak wisdom; / the meditation of my heart shall be understanding. / I will incline my ear to a proverb, / I will solve my riddle to the music of the harp" (NRSV, Ps 49:1–4).

Meditation/Journal: What type of music makes you aware of being in God? Is singing, playing, or listening the most helpful? When do you stop singing, playing, or listening to music? Why?

Prayer: Just as music—sung, played, or listened to—surrounds those singing, playing, or listening, so you, Most High God, surround people and make them aware that they exist in you. Hear every note I sing or play, and listen with me to the music I hear, and grant that one day I may praise you, in whom I live and move and exist, with music eternally. Amen.

House

Introduction: A celebration in honor of one's house—such as the date one moved into it, bought it, paid off its mortgage, etc.—is an opportunity to raise awareness that the home in which one lives exists in God, or, to put it another way, God lives in your house with you.[63] Today, a solitary may live in a house, an apartment, a condominium, a duplex, a cabin, or a hermitage. A hut in the desert is no longer able to take care of human needs. Solitaries need indoor plumbing, a bathroom, a bedroom, maybe an office, and maybe a guest room with the usual dining room or dinning nook and kitchen. Living alone in a cabin in the woods, while still done by a few people, is not the choice for a solitary life for most people. Modern conveniences—electricity, internet access, and a furnace/

---

63. For more on the sacredness of one's house, see Mark G. Boyer's *Home is a Holy Place: Reflections, Prayers and Meditations Inspired by the Ordinary* (Chicago: ACTA, 1997).

air conditioning unit—free the solitary for prayer, meditation, and journaling. A solitary may refer to his or her dwelling as a hermitage, a home where a hermit—a solitary—lives, but such a place today is built to cater to modern, basic human needs.

Biblically, the word *house* can designate a dynastic family—such as royalty, a large group—such as clan or tribe, or even an entire people—such as Israel. In some biblical books, *house* signifies a condition of life—such as slavery—or the Temple, God's dwelling place, in addition to referring to a physical structure in which people live. Archaeology has uncovered the fact that in general most biblical people, unless they were royalty, chiefs, or clan leaders, lived in a single-room house or a three-room house.

One of the more famous biblical accounts of living in a house is found in the narrative concerning Joseph in the HB (OT) book of Genesis. Joseph is sold into slavery to Ishmalites by his brothers. The slavers take him to Egypt, where one of Pharaoh's officials—Potiphar—buys him. "He ended up living in the home of his Egyptian master" (Gen 39:2). Potiphar recognized Joseph's abilities and put him in charge of all his personal affairs. Potiphar's unnamed wife took an interest in Joseph and tried to seduce him. Then, when Potiphar came home, she told him that Joseph had tried to seduce her. Of course, Potiphar believed her and had Joseph jailed (Gen 39:1–23).

Another interesting story involving a house is found in the HB (OT) book of Joshua. Joshua, who succeeds Moses as leader of the Israelites, sends spies to check out the land on the west side of the Jordan River before directing the Israelites to cross the river and claim the land. The spies "left and arrived at the house of a harlot named Rahab and stayed there" (Josh 2:1). After the king of Jericho hears about the spies, he sends word to Rahab to bring the men who came to stay the night in her house. She, however, took the men and hid them (Josh 2:1–24). Thus, she saved their lives. The author of CB (NT) Matthew's Gospel was so impressed by her deed, that he names Rahab in the family tree of Jesus. He writes, that Rahab was the mother of Boaz, who married Ruth, who gave birth to Obed, the father of Jesse, the father of King David (Matt

1:5–6). Thus, did the best little harlot house in Jericho get world-wide recognition, and Rahab became an ancestor of the Messiah!

Read: 2 Samuel 7:1–29

Scripture: ". . . [T]he word of GOD came to Nathan saying, 'Go and tell my servant David: This is GOD's word on the matter. You're going to build a "house" for me to live in? Why, I haven't lived in a "house" from the time I brought the children of Israel up from Egypt till now. All that time I've moved about with nothing but a tent'" (2 Sam 7:4–7).

Reflection: The narrative that follows David's anointing as king over all the tribes of Israel and his capture of Jerusalem and establishment of it as his capital city states: "David made the fortress city his home and named it 'City of David.' He developed the city from the outside terraces inward" (2 Sam 5:9). King Hiram of Tyre sent cedar timbers, carpenters, and masons to build a house for David (2 Sam 5:11). Sitting in his palace one day, David began to think out loud to his court prophet, Nathan: "Look at this: Here I am, comfortable in a luxurious house of cedar, and the Chest [Ark] of God sits in a plain tent" (2 Sam 7:2). Nathan understands that David is thinking about building a house for God, and so he thinks it is a good idea until the word of God comes to Nathan during the night and tells him otherwise.

Using the word *house* as a double entendre—a word having more than one meaning—God tells Nathan that he doesn't need a house; a tent is what he has lived in since the days of Egypt, and in a tent he prefers to stay! Then, God instructs Nathan to go to David and remind him that God is in charge! ". . . GOD himself will build you a house," states Nathan (2 Sam 7:11). While David has in mind a physical house (temple) for God, the divine has in mind a dynasty of kings in Judah that lasts until 587 BCE, when King Zedekiah is taken as a captive of war to Babylon by King Nebuchadnezzar.

God does not need a house, a temple, a church, etc. in which to live, because everything exists in him. That is why the house or apartment of a solitary can raise his or her awareness that he or she lives and moves and exists in his or her home in God. People need a physical structure in which to be protected from the elements, but God does not. A celebration in honor of one's home can raise the solitary's awareness that he or she indeed lives in God. In other words, the solitary's home is a place of worship, a place to meet God.

Psalm Response: "How lovely is your dwelling place, / O LORD of hosts! / My soul longs, indeed it faints / for the courts of the LORD, / my heart and my flesh sing for joy / to the living God. / Even the sparrow finds a home, / and the swallow a nest for herself, / where she may lay her young, / at your altars, O LORD of hosts, / my King and my God. / Happy are those who live in your house, / ever singing your praise" (NRSV, PS 84:1–4).

Meditation/Journal: What signs in your home remind you that you are in God or that God lives with you in your house? In what specific ways does your house remind you that you are in God?

Prayer: No house can contain you, O LORD, since all people and things exist in you. Grant that my home may be your dwelling place, and that I may live with you, Father, Son, and Holy Spirit, today, tomorrow, and eternally. Amen.

Generic Celebration

Introduction: A generic celebration is for anything not listed above. It may be the solitary's birthday, upon getting a new appliance or car, when a friend comes to visit, or some other event special to the solitary. The object of the celebration is a deeper awareness of being in God, "participation in the life of God" (2 Pet 1:4). In the words of the Lukan Jesus, "Keep your shirts on; keep the lights on!" (Luke 12:35) In other words, be ready for awareness to be raised at any time; and when the awareness arises, be thankful for it. The author of the First Letter of John puts it this way: "The God-begotten are also the God-protected. We know that we are held firm by God. And we know that the Son of God came so we could recognize and understand the truth of God—what a gift!—and we are living in the Truth itself, in God's Son, Jesus Christ" (1 John 5:19–20). Rami Shapiro, referring to the awareness of being in God as enlightenment, says, it is "[t]he realization that you and all life are a manifesting of nondual Aliveness called by many names: Mother, Kali, God, Brahman, Allah, Tao, YHVH, Aliveness, Nature, Great Spirit, etc."[64] Shapiro explains, "The only way to awaken to God is by realizing this Self [God] as your Self."[65] He adds, "The true You is God, birthless and deathless."[66] In other words, "You are God. . . . There is nothing that isn't God."[67] When people approach spirituality from a dualistic framework, that is, God is in heaven and I am on earth and I am on a search for God, Shapiro explains: "You don't find God, you meet God. You meet God when you meet people, animals, bugs, trees, rivers, and even poop. When you meet God, you are called upon to act godly: to treat everything with kindness and respect."[68] There are not many gods; there is but one God, who has many forms.[69] According to the First Letter of John, the Christian form is the Son of God, Jesus Christ.

Read: John 15:1–17

Scripture: "If you love me, show it by doing what I've told you. I will talk to the Father, and he'll provide you another Friend so that

---

64. Shapiro, "Roadside Assistance," *Spirituality and Health* 26:1 (2023) 8.

65. Shapiro, "Roadside Assistance," *Spirituality and Health* 26:1 (2023) 8.

66. Shapiro, "Roadside Assistance," *Spirituality and Health* 26:1 (2023) 9.

67. Shapiro, "Roadside Assistance," *Spirituality and Health* 26:1 (2023) 9.

68. Shapiro, "Roadside Assistance," *Spirituality and Health* 26:1 (2023) 9.

69. Shapiro, "Roadside Assistance," *Spirituality and Health* 26:1 (2023) 9.

you will always have someone with you. This Friend is the Spirit of Truth. The godless world can't take him in because it doesn't have eyes to see him, doesn't know what to look for. But you know him already because he has been staying with you, and will even be *in* you!" (John 14:15–17)

Reflection: The author of John's Gospel refers to the spiritual awareness of being in God using several different images or metaphors. The first, as can be seen in the three-verse passage above, is Friend. A friend is somebody who has a close personal relationship of mutual affection and trust with another. The Johannine Jesus identifies this friend with the Spirit of Truth, who cannot be seen by the ordinary person. This invisible friend is Spirit, the very one who gives his or her name to spirituality. Those who practice a solitary spirituality know for what to look. And just as the Johannine Jesus tells his followers, we already know the Spirit; not only does he or she stay with us, but the Spirit is in us, because we are in God and the Spirit is in God. How's that for an invisible Friend?!

Another image employed by the Johannine Jesus for the solitary spirituality that practices awareness of being in God is vine and branches. The Johannine Jesus says: "I am the Vine, you are the branches. When you're joined with me and I with you, the relation intimate and organic, the harvest is sure to be abundant" (John 15:15). Cynthia Bourgeault, referring to this spirituality as kingdom awareness, states, ". . . [I]t sees no separation—not between God and humans, not between humans and other humans."[70] The Johannine Jesus, according to Bourgeault, has in mind "mutual indwelling: I am in God, God is in you, you are in God, we are in each other."[71] "Live in me. Make your home in me just as I do in you," states Jesus (John 15:4). The NRSV renders "live in me" as "abide in me." It means exist, dwell, reside, lodge in him. ". . [I]f you make yourselves at home with me and my words are at home in you, you can be sure that whatever you ask will be listened to and

70. Bourgeault, "Love Flows."
71. Bourgeault, "Love Flows."

acted upon. This is how my Father shows who he is—when you produce grapes, when you mature as my disciples" (John 15:7–8).

The next image is found a few verses later. The Johannine Jesus states: "I've loved you the way my Father has loved me. Make yourselves at home in my love" (John 15:9). According to Bourgeault: "There is no separation between humans and God because of this mutual interabiding which expresses the indivisible reality of divine love. We flow into God—and God into us—because it is the nature of love to flow."[72] She adds: ". . . [T]he vine gives life and coherence to the branch while the branch makes visible what the vine is . . . . The whole and the part live together in mutual, loving, reciprocity, each belonging to the other and dependent on the other to show forth the fullness of love. That's Jesus' vision of no separation between human and Divine."[73] In her meditation, Bourgeault also develops the statement that "no separation between human and human" exists. She begins with the Markan and Matthean Jesus statement, "Love others as well as you love yourself" (Mark 12:31; Matt 22:39). According to Bourgeault, the love of neighbor is "a continuation of your very own being. It's a complete seeing that your neighbor is you. . . . [T]here are simply two cells of the one great Life. . . . And as these two cells flow into one another, experiencing that one Life from the inside, they discover that putting 'your life on the line for your friends' (John 15:13) is not a loss of one's self but a vast expansion of it—because the indivisible reality of love is the only True Self."[74]

The three images found in John's Gospel—invisible friend, vine and branches, and flowing love—offer much upon which for the solitary to reflect and to become more aware of being in, abiding in, or living in the divine. Such deeper spirituality is the result of any generic celebration on a special occasion.

Psalm Response, Option 1: "The heavens are telling the glory of God; / and the firmament proclaims his handiwork. / Day to day

72. Bourgeault, "Love Flows."

73. Bourgeault, "Love Flows."

74. Bourgeault, "Love Flows."

pours forth speech, / and night to night declares knowledge. / Let the words of my mouth and the mediation of my heart / be acceptable to you, / O LORD, my rock and my redeemer" (NRSV, Ps 1–2, 14).

Psalm Response, Option 2: "Bless the LORD, O my soul, / and all that is within me, / bless his holy name. / Bless the LORD, O my soul, / and do not forget all his benefits—/ who forgives all your iniquity, / who heals all your diseases, / who redeems your life . . . / who crowns you with steadfast love and mercy, / who satisfies you with good as long as you live / so that your youth is renewed like the eagle's" (NRSV, Ps 103:1–5).

Meditation/Journal: How has this celebration made you more aware of being in God? Is your solitary spiritualty dualistic? Explain. What form of God best raises your awareness of being (in) God? How is the Spirit your invisible friend? When have you experienced being in others and others being in you and become aware that all are (in) God?

Prayer: Everything around me, including me, shouts your presence, O God. Make this time of prayer acceptable to you. Open my heart and mind to deeper awareness of how this celebration brings me into your presence and into the presence of others who may or may not be here with me. Renew me in your love today, tomorrow, and forever. Amen.

3

Conclusion

S PIRITUALITY FOR THE SOLITARY—THOSE who live alone for whatever reason—is based on desire. The solitary desires to grow in awareness of being (in) God and actively seeks by practice to get better at recognizing the divine presence in everyone and everything. In other words, the solitary desires awareness of God's presence in water, food, oil, etc. Celebrations are based on the intention of the solitary to spark awareness, rest in it, reflect and meditate (and maybe journal) on it, and, in so doing, to further his or her spirituality, his or her connection to Spirit and other spirits. Biblical texts can help accomplish that, but so can other texts.

The solitary, like all other people, interprets texts automatically. This means that after reading a biblical text, you assign meaning to it, usually without knowing its context—what it meant for its intended and original audience thousands of years ago. In their naivete, many people adopt generic meanings for texts and events, such as "Everything happens for a reason," or "With great power comes great responsibility," or "Jesus died for my sins." Without understanding how interpretation works or the fact that biblical texts represent the author's interpretation of an event, a negative view of spirituality easily becomes operative. What did Jesus think his death meant? We don't have an answer to that question because no one asked him, or, if someone did, his answer was not recorded. Thus, most meaning assigned to Jesus' death is negative; it is about forgiving sins.

What about a positive approach to spirituality? If spirituality is about the ongoing process of actively raising awareness of being in God's presence, then Jesus' life, death, and resurrection can inform spirituality about living, dying, and rising and about trusting God. A positive solitary spirituality that has little to do with sin, Satan, devils, etc. and everything to do with being in the presence of Jesus' God not only informs but sparks change in behavior. The focus is on living life in God to the full. Compassion and charity become responses to such spirituality. Instead, all that Christians supposedly stand against gets buried in the dung heap of sin, sex, etc. Once set free from the negative, a positive spirituality begins to emerge. People are set free from having to earn salvation by being good and avoiding evil. Fear is removed, and the fullness of spiritual life is embraced.

What gives meaning to modern solitary spirituality is not happiness; it is tragedy. We remember the tragic moments of life because we respond to them. Tragedy—sudden and unexpected death, school shootings, one country invading another—affects spirituality because we have to assign meaning—the minimum interpretation being chaos—to what happened. We remember few of the happy moments because we do not have to respond to them. We have to process tragedy, digest it, and deal with it. That is exactly what people were doing thousands of years ago; they recorded their interpretations in what has become biblical literature. For example, the author of the oldest gospel—Mark—had to give meaning to Jesus' death on a cross. Tragedy is where that author found an abundance of spiritual life. He leads the reader to wonder if finding God in the very place where God was not supposed to be—on a cross—isn't motivation enough for becoming aware that we are (in) God and we don't have to attempt to find the divine in whom we live and move and have our being. Solitary spirituality is a lifetime process of opening to the possibility that who we have always thought God to be may not be God at all. Also, solitary spirituality is a lifetime process through meditation of raising awareness that we have found the divine, and God has found us, and we are one throughout life here and hereafter.

John Roberto writes, "People set out to live their lives, expressing themselves fully."[1] He accurately states the goal of such a spiritual life: "The point is to become yourself, to use yourself completely—all your skills, gifts, and energies—in order to make your vision manifest. You must withhold nothing. You must, in sum, become the person that you started out to be, and enjoy the process of becoming."[2] By becoming yourself, you also become aware that you are (in) God. Your spiritually true self is God. As you live your life, expressing yourself more and more, you are manifesting God.

Frank Hasel cautions, "The holy can easily become common when we deal with it daily"[3] He stresses, "The most important devotional exercise is still daily time spent alone with God in reflection on Scripture and in prayer."[4] He states, "You cannot hasten spiritual insights."[5] He also offers this advice: "[The] inward digestion of the biblical truth is connected in significant ways with undisturbed time devoted to reading and applying the Word of God to our lives. This must be accompanied by prayer."[6] Digesting biblical truth requires meditation, journaling, contemplation, *Lectio Divina*—whatever works best for the spiritually solitary.

"We have at our disposal our own personal story, given to us by God and inspired with wisdom and symbols and teaching that

1. Roberto, *Digital*, 110.
2. Roberto, *Digital*, 110–11.
3. Hasel, "Spiritual," 10.
4. Hasel, "Spiritual," 11.
5. Hasel, "Spiritual," 12.
6. Hasel, "Spiritual," 12.

it is our task to ponder and unravel," states Alice Camile.[7] In a vein similar to Roberto above, Camile cautions: "People who don't stop and contemplate their personal journeys, as we know, are doomed to walk in circles through the same bleak scenarios until they do. All the wisdom of the ages is available to us—including the near and present revelation of our experiences as confirmation of the whole. No blessing is complete until we ponder its meaning and take it to heart."[8]

This is why celebrations are so important for the enhancement of the spirituality of the solitary. Celebrations raise awareness of being in God; reflecting and meditating on personal experiences, expressions of self, is where we begin. Spending time in the sunshine, admiring the clear blue sky and the puffy white clouds floating within it, or sitting in a room with moonshine streaking through a window are personal spiritual experiences and expressions of self awaiting reflection, meditation, and prayer. Likewise, reading a good book that draws you in and helps you interpret your life is matter for meditation. Watching a single DVD or a series of them enables you to plumb the depth of characters, even as you are seeking your own depth of character in God. Stopping to reflect on the handwritten words in a letter or card received recently in the mail or an e-mail, whose words seem to touch us in some way, nourishes the solitary's spirituality.

God, who is existence itself, does not bring anyone or anything into being without keeping it in being. Thus, whatever exists cannot not exist or go out of existence. Every person, tree, sheep, cow, dog, cat, etc. never ceases to exist. Death changes life—it doesn't erase it. Death changes life into total spirit. When those pursuing solitary spirituality stop separating, stop the duality of polar opposites in our world, we begin to experience that all is one in God. All being exists in Being; all existence exists in Existence. All are spirit in the process of spirituality, forever expressing self, which is simultaneously an expression of God. As Alexander

7. Camile, *Transforming: A*, 30.

8. Camile, *Transforming: A*, 30.

Turpin states, ". . . [W]e can access the unlimited God anywhere, anytime."[9] No one is able to do this as well as a solitary.

STOP/MEDITATE/JOURNAL

1. Characterize your desire for God as a solitary. Is your spirituality positive or negative? Explain.

2. What texts do you use to spark awareness of being (in) God?

3. How does tragedy give meaning to your life? List specific tragedies and write the meaning of each.

4. How has your conception of God changed over the years? after reading this book?

5. During the day, when do you spend time reflecting on Scripture and praying? Name one recent spiritual insight.

6. What events have you experienced personally that have enhanced your solitary spirituality?

7. Identify the duality in your spirituality. What can you do about it?

9. Turpin, "Of Pandemics," 335.

Bibliography

Alexopoulos, Stefanos, and Maxwell E. Johnson. *Introduction to Eastern Christian Liturgies.* Collegeville, MN: Liturgical, 2022.

Anderson, Kevin. "Thistle Seed and This'll Seed." *Spirituality and Health* 24:5 (2021) 18–19.

Anderson, Kevin. "The Soul of Therapy." *Spirituality and Health* 24:6 (2022) 10–11.

Anthony, Cara L. "The Sacraments and Liturgies of the Street." *Worship* 95:4 (October 2021) 316–34.

Benedict of Nursia. *St. Benedict's Rule for Monasteries.* Translated by Leonard J. Doyle. Collegeville, MN: Liturgical, 1948.

Bergin, Liam. "Saving Water." *Worship* 96:2 (April 2022) 106–23.

Bourgeault, Cynthia. "Love Flows." https://cac.org/daily-meditations/love-flows-2022-12-30/.

Boyer, Mark G. *An Abecedarian of Sacred Trees: Spiritual Growth through Reflections on Woody Plants.* Eugene, OR: Wipf and Stock, 2016.

———. *Divine Presence: Elements of Biblical Theophanies.* Eugene, OR: Wipf and Stock, 2017.

———. *From Contemplation to Action: The Spiritual Process of Divine Discernment Using Elijah and Elisha as Models.* Eugene, OR: Wipf and Stock, 2018.

Boylan, M. Eugene. *Difficulties in Mental Prayer.* Notre Dame, IN: Ave Maria, 2010.

Boyle, Gregory. *Tattoos on the Heart: The Power of Boundless Compassion.* New York: Free, 2010.

Branscombe, Mara. "A Ritual-Full Life." *Spirituality and Health* 25:4 (2022) 38–39.

Braxton, Donald. "Religion Promises but Science Delivers: The Transhumanist Wager." *The Fourth R* 34:3 (2021) 3–9, 16.

Camile, Alice. *This Transforming Word: Cycle A.* Chicago: ACTA, 2013.

———. *This Transforming Word: Cycle C.* Chicago: ACTA, 2015.

Casey, Michael. *Balaam's Donkey.* Collegeville, MN: Liturgical, 2019.

Catechism of the Catholic Church. Washington, DC: United States Catholic Conference, Inc.—Libreria Editrice Vaticana, 1994.

Cathcart, Thomas. *There is no God and Mary is His Mother: Rediscovering Religionless Christianity*. Minneapolis, MN: Fortress, 2020.

Chu, Paul Joseph. "Expanding the Catholic Imagination: Chaste Perception." *Listening: Journal of Communication Ethics, Religion, and Culture* 54:3 (2019) 172–77.

The Didache. Translated by Kirsopp Lake. https://www.bc.edu/content/dam/files/research_sites/cjl/sites/partners/cbaa_seminar/didache.htm.

Ehle, Mary A. *Anointed for Discipleship*. Chicago, IL: Liturgy Training, 2019.

Ehrman, Bart D., and Zlatko Plese. *The Apocryphal Gospels*. New York: Oxford University Press, 2011.

Gaillardetz, Richard R. "Loving and Reforming a Holy yet Broken Church." *Worship* 97:1 (2023) 62–81.

Goldberg, Philip. "Holy Places Everywhere." *Spirituality and Health* 23:5 (2020) 24–25.

———. "Namaste: Let's Keep It After the Pandemic." *Spirituality and Health* 24:3 (2021) 12–13.

"The Gospel of Thomas." Translated by Simone Gathercole. In *The Apocryphal Gospels*, 45–70. United Kingdom: Penguin Random House, 2021.

Hansen, Michael. *The First Spiritual Exercises: Four Guided Retreats*. Notre Dame, IN: Ave Maria, 2013.

Hasel, Frank M. "The Spiritual Life of the Pastor." *Ministry* 95:1 (2023) 10–12.

Hiesberger, Jean Marie, ed. *The Catholic Bible: Personal Study Edition, The New American Bible*. New York: Oxford University Press, 2007.

Hopkins, Gerard Manly. "God's Grandeur." https://hopkinspoetry.com/poem/gods-grandeur/.

Hubl, Thomas. "Lean into Wisdom." https://spiritualityhealth.com/articles/2020/08/17/collective-trauma-thomas-hubl.

Hurd, Bob. "Rahner and Chauvet on Sacrament as Symbolic Mediation." *Worship* 95: 4 (2021) 300–315.

"Incense as a Timer." https://supernatural.com/blogs/news/the-benefits-of-incense#:~:text=In%20many%20religious%20practices%2C%20burning,for%20inner%20and%20outer%20journeys.

Kelly, Jean P. "Word by Word." *U.S. Catholic* 84:4 (2019) 45–46.

Kiesling, Stephen. "The New American Love Revolution: A Conversation with Marianne Williamson." *Spirituality and Health* 21:6 (2018) 62–67.

———. "Personal Accountability in Chaos: An Interview with James Hollis." *Spirituality and Health* 23:4 (2020) 46–52.

Klussman, Kristine. "What's Your Why?" *Spirituality and Health* 24:3 (2021) 38–40.

Lohfink, Gerhard. *Between Heaven and Earth: New Explorations of Great Biblical Texts*. Translated by Linda M. Maloney. Collegeville, MN: Liturgical, 2022.

———. *Prayer Takes Us Home: The Theology and Practice of Christian Prayer*. Translated by Linda M. Maloney. Collegeville, MN: Liturgical, 2020.

Maher, Dennis. "Soul and Spirit at Westar." *The Fourth R* 34:3 (2021) 10–14.

Malloy, Richard G. "The World Made Digital." *U.S. Catholic* 73:12 (December) 2008 12–17.

McColman, Carl. *Answering the Contemplative Call: Five Steps on the Mystical Path*. Charlottsville, VA: Hampton Roads, 2013.

McKenzie, John L. *Dictionary of the Bible*. Milwaukee: Bruce Publishing, 1965.

Nepo, Mark. "Our Walk in the World: Fitting Things Together." *Spirituality and Health* 22:6 (2019) 82–83.

Oakes, Edward T. *A Theology of Grace in Six Controversies*. Grand Rapids, MI: William B. Eerdmans, 2016.

O'Day, Gail R. and David Petersen, eds. *The Access Bible: New Revised Standard Version with the Apocryphal/Deuterocanical Books Updated Edition*. New York: Oxford University Press, 2011.

"Our Father—ELLC." https://liturgytools.net/2010/09/our-father-ellc.html.

"Our Father—ICEL–1973." https://liturgytools.net/2010/09/our-father-icel-1973.html.

Paintner, Christine Valters. *The Soul of a Pilgrim: Eight Practices for the Journey Within*. Notre Dame, IN: Sorin, 2015.

Petersen, Meggen Watt. "Working to Stay Here: An Interview with Mirabi Bush." *Spirituality and Health* 21:5 (2018) 60–64.

Peterson, Eugene H. *The Message: Catholic/Ecumenical Edition—The Bible in Contemporary Language*. Chicago, IL: ACTA, 20123.

Poust, Mary DeTurris. *Everyday Divine*. New York, NY: Alpha, 2012.

Robbins, Jeffrey. "Dispatches: The New in the Old." *The Fourth R* 35:5 (2022) 25.

Roberto, John, ed. *Digital Ministry and Leadership in Today's Church*. Collegeville, MN: Liturgical, 2022.

Rohr, Richard. "A Big Experiment." Center for Action and Contemplation. August 16, 2019. https://cac.org/daily-meditations/a-big-experiment-2019-08-16/.

———. "Connecting to the Eternal." Center for Action and Contemplation. December 19, 2018. https://cac.org/daily-meditations/connecting-to-the-eternal-2018-12-19/.

———. "The DNA of Creation." Center for Action and Contemplation. December 6, 2020. https://cac.org/daily-meditations/the-dna-of-creation-2020-12-06/.

———. "Engaged Love." Center for Action and Contemplations. September 22, 2020. https://cac.org/daily-meditations/engaged-love-2020-09-22/.

———. "Fallow Time." Center for Action and Contemplation. November 12, 2019. https://cac.org/daily-meditations/fallow-time-2019-11-12/.

———. "Knowing Our Source." Center for Action and Contemplation. December 10, 2018. https://cac.org/daily-meditations/knowing-our-source-2018-12-10/.

———. "A Liminal Time." *The Mendicant* 10:2 (2020) 1, 5.

———. "Open Heart, Mind, and Body." Center for Action and Contemplation. December 9, 2018. https://cac.org/daily-meditations/open-heart-mind-and-body-2018-12-09/.

———. "Perceiving Reality." Center for Action and Contemplation. December 18, 2018. https://cac.org/daily-meditations/perceiving-reality-2018-12-18/.

———. "Politics: Old and New." Center for Action and Contemplation. November 20, 2019. http://cac.org/daily-meditations/politics-old-and-new-2019-11-20/.

———. "Practice: Contemplating Art." In "Art: Old and New: Weekly Summary." Center for Action and Contemplation. November 16, 2019. https://cac.org/daily-meditations/art-old-and-new-weekly-summary-2019-11-16/.

———. "Sustaining Awareness." Center for Action and Contemplation. December 20, 2018. https://cac.org/daily-meditations/sustaining-awareness-2018-12-20/.

———. "An Uncreated Spark." Center for Action and Contemplation. August 15, 2019. https://cac.org/daily-meditations/an-uncreated-spark-2019-08-15/.

———. *The Universal Christ: How a Forgotten Reality Can Change Everything We See, Hope For, and Believe*. New York: Convergent, 2019.

The Roman Missal: Study Edition. Collegeville, MN: Liturgical, 2010.

"*Rosarium Virginis Mariae*: On the Most Holy Rosary." In *The Liturgy Documents*: Volume 4: Supplemental Documents for Parish Worship, Devotions, Formation, and Catechesis, 525–50. Chicago: Liturgy Training, 2013.

Ryken, Leland, James C. Wilhoit, and Tremper Longman, eds. *Dictionary of Biblical Imagery*. Downers Grove, IL: InterVaristy, 1998.

Salkeld, Brett. *Transubstantiation: Theology, History, and Christian Unity*. Grand Rapids, MI: Baker Academic, 2019.

Scoby, Annmarie. "Keep Prayer in Mind." *U.S. Catholic* 83:5 (2018) 43–44.

Shapiro, Rami. "Roadside Assistance for the Spiritual Traveler." *Spirituality and Health* 22: 5 (2019) 14–15.

———. "Roadside Assistance for the Spiritual Traveler." *Spirituality and Health* 25:1 (2022) 8–9.

———. "Roadside Assistance for the Spiritual Traveler." *Spirituality and Health* 25:2 (2022) 11–12.

———. "Roadside Assistance for the Spiritual Traveler." *Spirituality and Health* 25:6 (2022) 8–9.

———. "Roadside Assistance for the Spiritual Traveler." *Spirituality and Health* 26:1 (2023) 8–9.

———. "Roadside Assistance in the Holy Land." *Spirituality and Health* 22:1 (2019) 46–50.

Sheed, Frank. *Knowing God: God and the Human Condition*. New York: Sheed and Ward, 1966.

Sheldrake, Philip. *The Spiritual Way: Classic Traditions and Contemporary Practice*. Collegeville, MN: Liturgical, 2019.

Sterckx, Roel. "'Of a Tawny Bull We Make Offering:' Animals in Early Chinese Religion." In *A Communion of Subjects: Animals in Religion, Science, and Ethics*, edited by Paul Waldau and Kimberley Patton, 259–72. New York: Columbia University Press, 2006.

Sutherland, Paul. "The Heart of Happiness." *Spirituality and Health* 25:4 (2022) 74–75.

———. "The Heart of Happiness." *Spirituality and Health* 25:6 (2022) 74–75.

Taft, Robert F. "Between Progress and Nostalgia: Liturgical Reform and the Western Romance with the Christian East; Strategies and Realities." In *A Living Tradition: On the Intersection of Liturgical History and Pastoral Practice*, edited by David A. Pitt, Stefanos Alexopoulos, Christian McConnell, 19–39. Collegeville, MN: Liturgical, 2012.

Tassi, Alma. "Five Questions with Erling Kagge." *Spirituality and Health* 22:3 (2019) 88.

Thornton, David. "*Lectio Intima.*" *Spirituality and Health* 22:2 (2019) 36–37.

Turpin, Alexander. "Of Pandemics and Divine Mysteries." *Worship* 95:4 (2021) 335–52.

Webb, Stephen H., and Alonzo L. Gaskill. *Catholic and Mormon.* New York: Oxford University Press, 2015.

Zimmerman, Joyce. *Worship with Gladness: Understanding Worship from the Heart.* Michigan: William B. Eerdmans, 2014.

Recent Books by Mark G. Boyer
published by Wipf & Stock

Nature Spirituality: Praying with Wind, Water, Earth, Fire

A Spirituality of Ageing

Weekday Saints: Reflections on Their Scriptures

Human Wholeness: A Spirituality of Relationship

A Simple Systematic Mariology

Praying Your Way through Luke's Gospel and the Acts of the Apostles

An Abecedarian of Animal Spirit Guides: Spiritual Growth through Reflections on Creatures

Overcome with Paschal Joy: Chanting through Lent and Easter—Daily Reflections with Familiar Hymns

Taking Leave of Your Home: Moving in the Peace of Christ

An Abecedarian of Sacred Trees: Spiritual Growth through Reflections on Woody Plants

Divine Presence: Elements of Biblical Theophanies

Fruit of the Vine: A Biblical Spirituality of Wine

Names for Jesus: Reflections for Advent and Christmas

Talk to God and Listen to the Casual Reply: Experiencing the Spirituality of John Denver

Christ Our Passover Has Been Sacrificed: A Guide through Paschal Mystery Spirituality—Mystical Theology in The Roman Missal

Rosary Primer: The Prayers, The Mysteries, and the New Testament

From Contemplation to Action: The Spiritual Process of Divine Discernment Using Elijah and Elisha as Models

Love Addict

All Things Mary: Honoring the Mother of God—An Anthology of Marian Reflections

Shhh! The Sound of Sheer Silence: A Biblical Spirituality that Transforms

What is Born of the Spirit is Spirit: A Biblical Spirituality of Spirit

Very Short Reflections—for Advent and Christmas, Lent and Easter, Ordinary Time, and Saints—through the Liturgical Year

Living Parables: Today's Versions

My Life of Ministry, Writing, Teaching, and Traveling: The Autobiography of an Old Mines Missionary

300 Years of the French in Old Mines: A Narrative History of the Oldest Village in Missouri

Journey into God: Spiritual Reflections for Travelers

Monthly Entries for the Spiritual but not Religious through the Year: Texts, Reflections, Journal/Meditations, and Prayers for the Spiritual but not Religious

The Shelbydog Chronicles by Shelby Cole as Recorded by Mark G. Boyer: A Novel

Four Catholic Pioneers in Missouri: Lamarque, Kenrick, Fox, and Hogan: Irish Missionaries and Their Supporter

Smothered with Inexhaustible Mercy: An Anthology of Poems

www.ingramcontent.com/pod-product-compliance
Lightning Source LLC
Chambersburg PA
CBHW060817050726
47601CB00013B/81